Trumped
By
Sovereignty

JUGGLING FAITH, HEALING, AND SUBMISSION
TO GOD'S PERFECT PLANS

By Sara Stophel

Endorsements

Knowledge comes when we accumulate facts. Wisdom comes when we go through the fire. But divine wisdom is available to us when we can learn inspiring lessons from others who have been through the fire. Sara Stophel has been through the fire in her own life in ways very few of us will experience. I have known her family for many years and was an observer for at least part of the journey as Sara went through the fire. Through this book, she has lessons to teach us all. Read, learn, and grow.

Jim Stovall
Emmy Award winner and author of the bestseller,
"The Ultimate Gift"

It is their story – Chuck's story and her story. It is the story of cruel suffering, unspeakable disappointment, and premature death, but it is so much more than that. It is the story of great faith often mixed with fear, anger, and unbelief. And it is the story of God's faithfulness. In the end, God's love and Sara's faith triumph. "Trumped By Sovereignty" is a must read for anyone who has ever struggled to understand God's inscrutable ways.

Richard Exley
Best-selling author, "The Rhythm of Life"
and "The Making of a Man"

I was drawn in from the first page and read the entire book in two sessions. Sara is real, funny and refreshing. It is "deep waters" and a heart-felt message. Her journey of hope, testing and perseverance cuts to the core with a fanciful flare done with her "glass overflowing" attitude. "Trumped by Sovereignty" is a must read!

Lauren Kitchens Steward
National Radio Personality,
College Professor and Motivational Speaker

I have known the Stophels for over twenty years as their pastor and friend. I was confident that even though they were severely tested, their love and dependence on the Lord would sustain them through the many unanswerable questions they faced.

Like Sara and Chuck, all of us discover the Christian life is filled with unexpected twists and turns which can challenge our peace as well as our faith, but we also discover that no matter what happens the Lord is there with us!

Sara's journey is a testimony of the miraculous love of God. His faithfulness is exalted in this book…through healing and pain; through abundance and need; through life and death. I pray that her honesty and transparency, which have been used by the Lord to help many people, will help you too! "Trumped By Sovereignty" is a beautiful reflection of a strong woman who has discovered that the source of her strength is nothing more or less than the always dependable hand of God.

Greg Davis, Senior Pastor
Christian Chapel

Trumped By Sovereignty: Juggling faith, healing, and submission to God's perfect plans
Copyright © 2016—Sara Stophel
ISBN 978-0-9892257-5-5

Printed in the United States
Published by
Paladin Publishing
P. O. Box 700515
Tulsa, OK 74170 U.S.A.

Project development by PriorityPR Group & Literary Agency – www.prioritypr.org

Text Design: Lisa Simpson

Acknowledgements

I would like to thank the Academy of Believers who stood with us through all 200+ pages of the stories you are about to read. You are the Hands and Feet of Jesus, and your fingerprints are on my heart forever.

Butt Kickers, that's you…so faithful to follow our posts and so faithful to pray for God's intervention. Thank you.

Little Light House staff…you are the best pray-ers and givers EVER! I'm proud to be a part of your team!

Christian Chapel, you are our family. Thank you for serving and loving us, and for welcoming us back home!

Ed and Marilyn, there just aren't words to express what you did for me that first year following Chuck's change of address. I love you more than I can say.

To my Mazzio's group, Carol and Stuart, John and Felicia, Kathryn and Stan, (and on occasion Marilynda, and John and Toni!) I love you all so much! Thank you for asking, listening, hugging (even though I'm not a hugger!) crying, praying, laughing, and lunching with us for so many years!

Kathryn and Stan…you've gone way above and beyond. How do I thank friends who've given up vacation time to sit at a hospital, or sleep in a "recliner" next to Chuck so I could get a good night's sleep? How do I express gratitude to friends who've gone out of their way to make sure I was getting through another day? And how on EARTH could there BE enough "thank you's" for the time and effort you've put into this book?!!? I love you both so much!

Sue, Ann, and Jane, I love you and am blessed to be called your little sister. Mom, you've done way more than I could mention in a paragraph; thank you for being here for us and for sharing a home with us. I love you!

Charles, Barbara, and Nicole, I could NOT have asked for better in-laws. Thank you for sharing your Chuck with me, and for all you still do that reminds us...even while Chuck is away, we're still yours.

Creston, Nikolai, and Asher...you are my heart and my loves. You are beautiful, daily reminders of the amazing man God gave me. I am so proud of the men of God you have grown to be. Keep living out your stories, to the glory of God!

Chuck, I miss being your Princess! May this book be a reflection of the wonderful man you were. Until we meet again, Your Sara.

Table of Contents

A Song of New Hope

A Song of Grief

A New Song

A Song of Purpose

Foreword

✦

"There are far better things ahead than any we leave behind."

C. S. Lewis

Rango had been abandoned, but not on purpose. Though he had been a well-loved pet chameleon, fate found him tumbling from a moving car, and now tough situations were facing him. He made some poor choices in this new wild life he'd discovered, and now running away seemed like the only answer. In the animated movie by the same title, Rango ends up in the small town of Dirt. The proverbial wise owl shows up to advise his new friend. "Rango, you can't run out on your own life story." That line has crossed my mind many times these last several years. I sure have wanted to run out on *my* life story!

Let me introduce myself. I am a follower of Jesus, a mom of three amazing boys, a baby sister, and a daughter to my feisty mother! My newest hat is that of widow. Looking back, my whole life has been spent trying to find God's Truth in the midst of reality; trying to understand faith while watching sovereignty unfold. For example, fervent prayers were uplifted for years, yet diabetes continued its war against my sister's body. Years later, and with all the faith I could muster, I asked God to heal my husband's failing heart. But instead, God gave him a transplanted heart which we celebrated each of the next seventeen years. Then in January 2011, along with my boys, I prayed and hoped that God would exchange whole and healthy cells for the cancerous cells that were taking my husband, Chuck's life, but God chose June of 2012 to heal him in Heaven.

11

At the memorial service honoring my husband's life, I challenged my children (and myself) to live out the scripture, 2 Corinthians 1:3-4. Following is my Saraphrased version, since the Apostle Paul is king of the run-on sentence!

> *Praise be to the God and Father of our Lord Jesus Christ; He's the Father of compassion and the God of all comfort. He comforts us in all our troubles so that we can comfort others in the same way we have received comfort from God.*

I hope and pray that my story of pain and peace, anger and joy, fear and faith...expressed transparently, in scripture and an occasional four-letter word, will help you find what I'm finally finding myself ~ God's kind of Truth. If you feel like Rango, you're not alone. If you are wondering how faith and sovereignty can possibly work in tandem...join the crowd. But, by the blood of the Lamb and the words of our testimonies, we WILL overcome! (Revelation 12:11).

Sara's Secret

❧

"I'm somewhere between skinny jeans and granny panties."
Unknown

The answer is five. Five loooong trips to and from the mall. Most of us have experienced it at one time or another…some sort of crisis that takes priority over the everyday duties and needs of life. For me, there were about eighteen months of crisis living…and that, at the tail end of eighteen years of waiting for the other shoe to drop. Not EVERY day was traumatic during that whole time; I just learned how to live cautiously…still faithful, yet with my built-in Truster never quite letting down its guard.

Consequently, the house got a little disorganized. The grass grew taller than we generally would have allowed and the weeds along with it. The oil in the car wasn't changed on time…maybe not at all during those last eighteen months…and me, being the Mom of the family…well, it's just normal to take care of the rest of the gang first. Not being a martyr…it just comes with being a mom! So what am I getting at? I'll just say it: I needed to get rid of my worn-out undergarments and start over! I hate to admit this, but it was getting bad…when you get to a point that you might have to wear two pair of panties to make one good one…well, you've waited too long to shop! It just wasn't important all of those months!

After Chuck left for his new home in Heaven, I made my way to the mall. I walked all over the lingerie department…and then went home with nothing. A few weeks passed, and I took another shot at it. J. C. Penney's, Victoria's Secret, Macy's…home. Nothing. God forbid, were I to get in an accident wearing undies that were hanging by a lacy thread! Pretty sure my mother would have had to move out of town had that happened!!!

By the fourth trip to the mall it became apparent that the reason I continued to return home empty-handed was that I wasn't sure what kind of underwear a widow wears. There was no need to have pretty colors, or wear a lacy camisole. Nobody would see my bras or nighties, and besides, maybe it's not appropriate to wear silk anymore. At the same time…I was NOT purchasing any panties that resemble a pillowcase with leg holes! One more failed shopping day…and another couple months of wearing a bra with the wire poking through the side and into my armpit!

Well, I finally did it. I came home with new undergarments…not the kind for grannies, and not the kind for a newlywed…but something that's NOT falling apart…and something in which I can feel pretty and feminine. My "girls" may not be like twin fawns of a gazelle that browse among the lilies…but at least they have a home that's secure now! This grieving, this being single thing, goes much deeper and further than for what anyone ever prepared me. I knew I'd grieve more for my children than even for myself. I expected some tearful nights and an occasional moment of anger at life's course. But nobody ever said I'd have trouble buying underwear! As was predicted, it has become easier with time. Looking back, I'm able to see a thread of God's handiwork in and through even those days when underwear was the biggest challenge of the day! He's been weaving a story… and apparently, sections of it are stitched with silk and lace!

Songs of Origins

A Princess in Her Castle

❧

"Deep in every heart slumbers a dream,
and the couturier knows it: every woman is a princess."

Christian Dior

Growing up, our home was my castle. At least it was in my mind. We had plenty of room for the four Rinehart girls and always had SOMEONE else living there who needed help. Not sure how it happened, but at some point or another, living with us were teen prostitutes, alcoholics, druggies, and a man who embezzled from the Denver Broncos! My parents were not in ministry per se, but always felt the call of the Lord to open our spacious home to those "someones" who had made poor choices, costing them the privilege of living with their own families. Somewhere in the mix we also had one wonderful, Christian exchange student from Switzerland who stayed five years! Looking back, I can't believe my parents, raising four daughters, opened their home to total strangers, especially men! But we were never harmed, and we made friends with most all of the folk who needed a place of refuge.

My castle was surrounded by a perfect green blanket of Bentgrass planted lovingly by my dad…it's the kind of grass used on the "greens" at a golf course. It was like carpeting and looked especially lovely around the turquoise waters of our in-ground swimming pool. To one side of the pool was every kind of flowering plant and vegetable, in every color; to the other side, a strawberry garden, leveled like a tower with a sprinkler coming out at the top. It was a beautiful pyramid of green and red, with a tinge of yellow from little Max, who climbed to the top to "mark" his territory! Strawberries somehow lost their appeal to me! Just *behind* the pool were a few marijuana plants my sister sneaked in, but my dad didn't recognize those! My dad loved working in the garden and it showed. The back of the house faced south, but if I leaned over the castle balcony just a little, I could see a lighted cross on the foothills of the Rocky Mountains. I LOVED that cross. It had been placed there by a funeral home and was made up of humongous light bulbs that, from Denver, appeared as a single cross. To me, that was like God showing He was always around, and whenever I needed to, I could see Him there.

My home was a castle because, well, I was a princess. I am the youngest of the four girls, and being nearly six years younger than the closest one, I benefited as both the youngest and as an only child. I was very shy, insecure about myself in so many ways…BUT, inside I knew I was special to God for some reason. I didn't have a lot of friends after having moved in fifth grade to another part of town, and pretending to be a princess was good enough entertainment for me much of the time. It was a safe and secure home life, one built strong with very few cracks in the mortar.

It's funny how things that mean so little as an adult can, during childhood, be a little crack in the sure foundation of life. For me, the crack was a scar down the middle of my chest. I'd been born with a VSD, Ventricular Septal Defect. Apparently that's not uncommon; however, in most cases the hole closes up on its own in short time. Mine did not. The goal was to reach a healthy weight in order to have surgery to repair the hole. Gaining weight was a much more difficult job in those days! So in the meantime, I was pretty fragile and tired easily. While living in Wisconsin, our home was close enough to the elementary school that I was supposed to be a "walker";

however, making that two-block trip was way too tiring and as my parents both worked, I rode a taxi to school! A taxi every day!

After kindergarten, we moved to Colorado for my dad to open a new branch of the Roth Young Personnel Employment Agency. Who knew moving to Denver could be so hard on an already overworked little heart? Before long, my chest began to swell and my parents were told the mile-high altitude had caused my heart to become so enlarged that it would not recover to normal even after the hole was repaired. It would be like a rubber band that has been pulled and stretched until it finally loses all shape. Unfortunately, the pediatric cardiologists in Wisconsin were uninformed about the dangers we faced in moving to Denver's altitude and so the damage had been done.

My mom and dad were longtime churchgoers, but only in recent years had they really come to know there was a Jesus who was personal and involved in the lives of His followers. By summer of 1972, when I was six, I finally reached that target weight of twenty-six pounds, making it safe for open-heart surgery. Two weeks before heading to Mayo Clinic in Rochester, Minnesota, I was taken (along with my sister, Ann, who had been diagnosed with diabetes several years before) to a church meeting where the Happy Hunters were praying for the sick. Frances and Charles Hunter had prayed for and witnessed, according to their biographical website, the healings of people in the TRIPLE-DIGIT MILLIONS! Nothing happened that night for *us* as far as we knew, but to this day I remember Mrs. Hunter reaching out toward my mother's forehead, me in her arms. She simply said, "Jesus," and down we went! I "awakened" lying on the floor without a clue how we got there. Next to me were my dad and Ann. My dad looked up to find he was *under* the front pew of the church, his face red with embarrassment...someone could have seen the hole worn through the sole of his shoe!

July 12 was my surgery, after which the surgeon assured my parents that my heart was not enlarged at all! It seemed as though the prayers of that night brought about a healing none of us really knew was ours! God worked surgically, and evidently, in spite of our lacking faith and knowledge, miraculously! The Teflon patch was in place and I was going to be better than ever...only with a scar several inches long down the center of my chest...a sort of crack in the mortar in my safe and secure self. Somehow that shaped my self-regard for years. My sweet mother bought every concealer cream on the market for me; she shopped for swimwear and shirts that would not show that little pink scar. Not an easy assignment!

Medically, I was released with few restrictions. It would be important that my grade in Physical Education classes not be based on any kind of timed performance as the doctor did not want me to push beyond a comfortable kind of tired. If only they had known how well I'd play that card for the rest of my life!

Meanwhile, 2,000 miles away...

A Prince and His Miracle

❧

"All men are by nature equal, made all of the same earth by one Workman; and however we deceive ourselves, as dear unto God is the poor peasant and the mighty prince."

Plato

Charles Dewitt Stophel was born March 15, 1967, to...to no one. Well, he was born to an unmarried woman who had made the best choice to give her baby life. Actually, she didn't have the choice in those days to NOT give her baby life. Hummm...just sayin'!

"Baby Boy" was taken by the North Carolina Children's Home Society and placed for adoption. Charles and Barbara Stophel had completed their paperwork and home studies for adoption, and less than two months later, they received the news that there was a baby for them. If they hurried they could have him before the weekend! The rushing ensued and they made it just in time to meet their new baby boy...wearing a dress! The price for that adoption in 1967? Twelve empty bottles to replace the twelve bottles full of formula they were given to take home. On April 23, "Baby Boy" became "Chuck." The Stophel home was one of faith and Chuck grew in stature, wisdom, and favor with the Lord and people. Two years later, tiny sister Nicole was adopted to make their family complete.

When Chuck was seven, he began having pain in his neck and in the pits of his arms. He underwent various tests, poking and prodding while

21

weeks passed and symptoms grew more intense. At one point doctors made the decision to do a spinal tap in further search of answers. His mother requested she be in the room for that very painful test, and against medical advice, she was allowed. She held Chuck's right hand and told him Jesus would be holding the left. Then she sang, "In the Name of Jesus, in the Name of Jesus, this pain has got to flee...." With an army of nurses and doctors ready to hold him down, the needle began its way into his back. Chuck let out a little squeak, but never moved or cried again, and they never needed to hold him down! One of the most painful diagnostic tests performed, and on a tiny little boy. Such a great witness to the team gathered in the room that day; a mother's love and God's miraculous provision.

All of that done and still nothing was found to be the culprit. Before long, Chuck was walking bent over like an old man, pain having grown so much worse. Eventually, a biopsy was done, removing a lymph node from the top of each leg, and a very rare cancer was diagnosed. This cancer would grow throughout the whole body at once, but only attacking cells here and there making a biopsy only a shot in the dark. If the "right" cells were not tested, the results would return "unremarkable" or clear. Before long, the disease would have multiplied to the point it could not be controlled. There had been only six known cases in the southeastern United States and of them, no one had lived more than three years.

There was nothing easy about the news Dr. Miale had to offer. He sat Chuck down and offered him a dollar if he would learn to spell Lymphatic Histiocytosis! (He learned it, and for years, made use of that word to impress grown-ups, or to play Hangman!) The prognosis was bad. Three years, if that. Charles had recently lost his job, so they had no insurance, but thankfully, Chuck's case was considered as a "catastrophic illness" by the state of Florida, which meant they would provide care at no cost at a training hospital in Gainesville, a few hours away. No insurance, but faith. Deadly prognosis, but hope.

Chuck's mother was a beautician and although she loved his curly blond hair, after much prayer, she did something I do not recommend unless you are one who hears audibly from God. I'm fairly certain SHE meets the requirements! Barbara asked Chuck if he would prefer to undergo chemotherapy, which would cause his hair to fall out and would probably make him feel sick sometimes, but would make the cancer go away; OR, would he rather keep his hair but continue to feel sick and weak. So brave of her (and slightly crazy)! Seven-year-old Chuck went up to his room and contemplated for THREE hours! In the end, he decided he would let his momma cut his hair short, and would go on with the treatments. Whew! Chemo treatments were several hours away from their home in Tallahassee, so the trips became a sort of date for Mom and son time. For the first treatment, Chuck was wheeled in as he'd become too weak and bent over to walk. That day, though, he walked out upright! Every two weeks they made the trip, and every two weeks he'd spend the evening sick and vomiting. He swore the real reason for the vomiting was that he always watched "The Waltons" after chemo!

His mom and dad offered him every kind of cap or hat, but Chuck preferred the Kojak look. Yet kids can be bullies, and one day at school, an older boy walked by Chuck in the cafeteria, yanking out the last few strands of his hair on the way by. The PE coach grabbed that kid, threw him up against the wall, and told him if he ever touched Chuck again, he'd kill him! Faithfully, Barbara and Charles prayed and believed for healing for their son. Faithfully, Barbara stomped up the staircase, shouting at Satan, "You cannot have my son!!" Faithfully, communion was served to honor God as He worked His miracle in that little life...even when it was not yet seen.

After a year and a half of chemo, and symptoms under control, Dr. Miale ran a battery of extra tests. The cancer was gone! God had worked through medicine, but surely He worked in a miraculous way! Had those faithful prayers been the answer? The Bible says in Mark 11:23, whoever speaks to a mountain, telling it to be thrown into the sea, and has no doubt, *it will be done* for him. Chuck was the first person ever to survive lymphatic histiocytosis.

And so, God continued the weaving of our stories. Only He knew that in time our two half-woven tapestries would begin being stitched together. First, however, there were threads of experiences that needed to be woven into place from within our own families. One such thread seemed to me, to be less like silk and more like burlap...the weaving of which often hurt.

Paged in Tucson

❧

"Yesterday is history, tomorrow is a mystery, today is a gift of God, which is why we call it the present."

Bil Keane

On May 23, 1987, the Rinehart family gathered in Tucson for my sister Jane's wedding. Sue, the oldest, sang and played piano, Ann was the Matron of Honor, and I, another Bridesmaid. It was a pretty ceremony, but to me the day had been scarred from the start.

Ann was twenty-eight and diabetic, and by that time had been placed on a waiting list for a kidney transplant. She carried a pager at all times, but until the day it beeped, she would undergo twelve hours of dialysis each week. I went with her often and drove home as the dialysis was very draining. Ann would go in weighing 108 pounds and come out weighing 104 pounds. Her blood made its way through yards of tubing and machine filters and then back into her body minus the wastes. Being in Arizona for the wedding meant we were far from home in Denver, and far from the dialysis center for more days than usual. Her diet would have to be watched like a hawk.

When Ann woke up the morning of the wedding, she was so thirsty. As soon as the breakfast was placed on the hotel-room table, she gulped down an eight-ounce glass of orange juice in one breath. "Ann!!! You can't DO that!! That's all you get to drink today!" That memory was etched in my mind for years. Her shocked and disappointed face...nothing else to drink.

All. Day. Honestly, that seemed so mean, but I knew it was to protect her health. Really, it was God who seemed mean. As a matter of fact, there were a number of times I thought God missed His opportunity with Ann.

Diabetes had wreaked havoc on her body. Science was not as advanced as today, and blood sugars were so very difficult to control. Ann often had sores that refused to heal on her feet. Now she had a shunt in her arm, placed for what could be long-term dialysis, and IT seemed to be clogged more often than open. This long incision up her tiny, tender arm…tube underneath still visible…would not heal. I remember standing around her hospital bed one afternoon, holding hands ready to pray…once again…that the shunt would heal and the blockage would be removed so she could avoid another surgery scheduled for the following morning. Right there in the hospital room, her doctor, a Jewish man who never engaged himself in the "religious" things we did, offered up a prayer ALOUD with us!! "There it is!" I thought! "Now God will heal her arm for sure! Now He'll show Himself real and true!!" Nope. Morning came, shunt was still blocked, arm still infected. Surgery went on as scheduled. How could God miss that opportunity? Dr. Hutner would HAVE to have believed in our Jesus! There was no other way that arm would have healed overnight! But, it didn't heal, and I assumed he didn't ever believe either. Why doesn't God reveal Himself when given such an opportunity?

Jane's wedding happened without incident, but the following morning as we packed up to go home, Ann's beeper beeped! Craziness ensued! Before long, she and my mother were on a flight to Denver to receive a kidney transplant. The rest of us caught up as soon as we could. What a relief! No more dialysis! Surely God will show Himself now. Surely THIS will be her time to shine the miracles of Jesus! This is the beginning of her healed life! As for the rest of the family, a sense of relief. No more would a late night phone call cause our hearts to skip a beat.

The Two Shall Become One

❧

"A cord of three strands is not quickly broken."

Ecclesiastes 4:12

Almost a year later, Chuck and I met at Oral Roberts University in Tulsa, Oklahoma. I had auditioned to sing with a summer music ministry team, with whom Chuck had toured the previous year. For a number of reasons, the male vocalists on our team began dropping out, and eventually Chuck was invited back to ORU to sing with us for the summer. It ended up being Chuck and four girls! Charlie's Angels! The very night he arrived in Tulsa we had our first concert, and WE sang our first duet…"Jesus Never Fails." I'll be honest, I thought Chuck was cute! However, it was not until several weeks into our cross-country ministry trip that I found a real attraction to him…it was the night he first gave his testimony. Hearing his story of childhood cancer, faith and healing did something in me I'd never felt before. He was anointed, not an ordinary man…and suddenly, I wanted to be a part of the rest of his testimony!

As it turned out, my job on tour was Housing Director…which meant I arranged who stayed with whom each night while with host families. I had a rotating schedule so we'd all get to know one another, but on the occasion that a host family had room for both guys and gals, I'd always arrange that Chuck and I were included in the bunch! There would be dessert and chatting, and occasionally, an opportunity to pray and minister to a struggling family. Then, Chuck and I would stay up even later talking about whatever subject would keep us going just so we could be together.

While singing and speaking in Vancouver, a pastor asked permission to pray over our team before we ministered to his congregation later that evening. Strangely to me, he placed his hands on my head and professed, "You will have a mighty healing ministry." I was as open as I could be to whatever God would call me, but healing was the one thing that seemed out of my league. I STILL didn't know what I believed about healing myself... how would *I* minister in that way to others? I would keep my eye out for confirmations. He also declared that several of the team members would be married within the next year! (Four of us were, including our director, who married that pastor's secretary!)

The weeks passed and Chuck and I were clearly developing a fondness for one another. At some point I told him if he asked me out when we returned to Tulsa, I'd go..."even though there were several other guys who liked me back home!" (I was counting our exchange student from home, my cousin Danny...my dad!) Dating on tour is highly frowned upon, so we held it together until the bus hit the ORU parking lot at which time he asked me out!

We spent the next two nights out together, the first at a Christian rock concert where family friend and up-and-coming comedian, Steve Geyer, was opening for DeGarmo and Key. The next night, we attended an opera! Opposites attract! The rest is history. I'd found my prince and he, his princess. Chuck found a job at ORU so we could continue dating while I went back to classes in the fall. We had dreams of singing, speaking, and touring the world for Jesus; happy to live out of a suitcase, like we had these first months getting to know one another. Talk of marriage was in the works. Nothing lie ahead but time together and time to share all God had done in and through our lives!

A Dress for Another Occasion

*"Death never comes at the right time, despite what mortals believe.
Death always comes like a thief."*

Christopher Pike

It had been about nine months since Chuck and I began our courtship, so spending the five-week Christmas break separated made for long days for a young couple in love! It had become apparent that this relationship was going to be forever, and since it would be summer before I'd see family again, it seemed only logical to plan ahead. So, early one morning, my parents and I got up and were off to shop for a wedding dress! I wasn't engaged yet, but I was pretty sure it was coming...we had to take advantage of Christmas break! We spent the day in Phoenix, where they were living temporarily to help the Grands, trying on gown after gown, laughing, lunching, and eventually purchasing the first gown I had tried!

When we arrived home we found notes taped to the garage door and to the front door...and the answering machine blinking like a strobe light. Our hearts went from elation to devastation...my sister Ann did not wake up that day; her blood sugar read 8, with a normal count being 100. We were in shock. How could God have let my sister die? My parents took the first flight to Denver, while I stayed in Arizona to prepare the house for visitors due in a couple of days. That night Chuck called me, as usual, to chat about our days. After filling him in about Ann...and likely still in a state of shock...I hesitated, but then let him know we had purchased a

29

new dress that day. A long white one! Perhaps that made things a bit TOO easy for him! I think I was numb from the whole day's events. I had been so excited for what was to come, and then was suddenly so *grieved* for what was now to come. My day had been a whirl.

On January 6, I completed my round-trip ticket back to Tulsa with a six-hour layover to catch a flight to Denver for Ann's memorial service. It was during those six hours that Chuck got down on one knee and proposed! Timing is everything, and in most cases this would NOT be a good time. But for us, it was God's perfect time and brought about a source of joy for the coming months of wedding preparation as we grieved the loss of my sister.

My sister's death was just one more opportunity for me to ask God, "Why? How?" Another opportunity to shake my head at the wonder of God and His ways that were and are indeed higher than my own. Ann had been prayed for many times. Faithful prayers...the kind that you know, that you know, that you KNOW God will hear and answer in a miraculous way. Still, it seemed as though He always worked in another way completely, and now she was gone. My understanding of God and healing seemed further away than ever. Mulling around in my head were questions about faith and sovereignty, and how they could possibly work together.

Chuck and I married July 16, 1989, still dreaming of ministry, travel, babies, and a long life together. We each gained about thirty pounds working nights at J. C. Penney, then playing cards and eating brownies into the wee morning hours...so romantic! Before long, we both had real jobs, Chuck with Harrison House Publishing and I at Little Light House, a Christian development center for children with special needs.

By October of 1994 we had been blessed with two precious little boys. Charles Creston had just turned two, and tiny Irvin Nikolai merely five weeks. Nikolai came a month early by emergency C-section and was sent home with an apnea monitor, but he was growing stronger every day. Life seemed pretty perfect. Chuck had a job that could become a career, and I was now staying home with my two angels.

Funny, the scripture on our wedding invitation five years before read, "A cord of three strands is not quickly broken" (Ecclesiastes 4:12). There was no way to know how much that cord would be stretched in a very short time.

Your Turn

Take a moment to reflect on your origin. How have the days you've lived so far shaped who you are right now? Did your home provide a safe foundation, or were there cracks that still need repair?

_____

_____

_____

_____

_____

_____

_____

_____

_____

_____

_____

_____

Heart Songs

He'll Need a New Heart

❧

*"I will give you a new heart and put a new spirit in you; I will
remove from you your heart of stone and give you a heart of flesh.
And I will put my Spirit in you and move you to
follow my decrees and be careful to keep my laws."*

Ezekiel 36:26-27

NOVEMBER 1, 1994, JOURNAL ENTRY:

"Dear God,

*Chuck's parents went home today so we're…on our own. We're doing
okay – we're a little scared, but our faith is strong. In the last six weeks,
we've gone through an emergency C-section, infant CPR training, a
diagnosis of heart failure, and a subsequent heart attack. Dr. Ensley's
comments leave our minds swimming: 'Chuck could drop dead at any
moment. You're lucky he didn't already die in his sleep.' And if those
weren't bad enough, when Chuck's mom asked him to give us just one
good thing to keep hold of, he said he couldn't think of any. Good thing
we have You! AND… Dr. Ensley needs some bedside training! He's a
young 35-year-old cardiologist with a big job, but he's not You! Sheesh!
It's hard to believe a simple virus could have destroyed Chuck's 27-year-
old heart in just a matter of days…but that's what they tell us. We trust
You and know You've got this."*

35

This was the first entry in my journal following the crazy beginnings of our new normal. Chuck, along with most of his sales staff, had been experiencing an overall feeling of exhaustion. Assuming he had a common virus or infection, he saw whatever doctor was available to scribble a quick prescription and get him back on his feet. The routine check of vital signs for Chuck became a series of chest X-rays, blood tests, and Echocardiograms. The resident doctor, instead of scribbling ten days' worth of Penicillin, called another doctor in the Practice to help explain their findings. Cardiomyopathy. Likely, a virus had attacked his heart... much like they attack one's ears or sinuses. The senior doc confirmed... yes, Chuck's heart was failing, working at about fifteen percent capacity. Based on the diagnostic tests, heart transplantation was his only hope for survival. It seemed impossible to us. He was only twenty-seven years old and had walked several miles fund-raising for Little Light House just days before. We walked out with baby Nikolai in our arms, new heart meds in our hands, and a complete lack of understanding in our heads.

The following Sunday Chuck was scheduled to sing the offertory in church. Still practically asymptomatic, considering the severity of his condition, he went on with the plan. "There's not a victory without a fight. There's not a sunrise without a night." An eerie melody by Michael English. Our pastor announced to the congregation the news we had received early in the week. They prayed for us, and then Chuck walked off the stage and suffered a heart attack in the church parlor. Twenty-seven-year-old daddies of little boys aren't supposed to have heart attacks. And so, the not-so-real diagnosis from days before was suddenly reality. Had we known what the future held, I can't say we'd have signed up for it, but then again, Chuck was the optimist of ALL optimists! He was certain everything would be okay. This was just a hiccup through which we would walk and grow. "There's not a purchase without a cost. There's not a Crown...without a Cross."

You, Light up My Life...CLEAR!

❦

"God is too wise to be mistaken. God is too good to be unkind.
So when you don't understand, when you can't see His plan,
when you can't trace His hand...Trust His heart."

Babbie Mason

By early 1995 the symptoms of Chuck's heart failure had become very clear. I will never forget being awakened to the sound of him darting out of bed gasping for air. The symptoms of his heart pumping at only 15 percent were catching up with him. Work was becoming more difficult. To our complete amazement, his boss called him in to announce he had developed a disability plan in Chuck's honor…he would be retired at full pay and benefits until he was well! What?!? That was the first (and perhaps the only!) time God answered a prayer before we had even thought to ask!

After a twenty-four hour heart monitor test, it was determined Chuck would need a defibrillator implanted for the very likely event that his heart jumped out of a safe rhythm. He was delighted to have it done on Valentine's Day…being a heart procedure and all! A defibrillator…you know the one; you've seen it on Grey's Anatomy: "CLEAR!!" and as Chuck would say, "It shocks the snot out of you!" Thirty days later it did just that.

We were visiting at the kitchen table when his eyes began to roll back. Slowly, he folded in half toward the table and…BANG! He sat up, confused as to what had happened, wondering if smoke rings were coming from his ears! I knew what had happened, I heard it, and I saw its effects. For months any loud sound…a closing door, a soda can being opened, even the claps of my little boy's hands sounded like a defibrillator to me. A few moments later Chuck realized there was a buzzing in his chest…a charge was building up. He always said NASA was counting down, "10, 9, 8…" and BANG!…another shock came just as he was dialing family to pray. With the jolt, the phone flew into the wall and it wasn't "Glory Hallelujah" that came from his mouth! We arrived at the hospital before the third shock, "Everyone stand clear, the monitor is predicting…." BANG! It was then we were told Chuck would stay in Cardiac Intensive Care until he got a new heart or he died. His biggest concern? He was certain our two-year-old Creston would someday be asked what he remembered his daddy's last words to be…"Daddy said, Dammit!" He was still able to laugh and joke, that was just Chuck's way. For me, it was the worst day of my life.

Shoving the Gospel

❧

"I may not sing like the angels. I may not preach like Paul. But I know I've been given the greatest gift of all, a new heart."

Michael W. Smith [1]

Chuck performed that Michael W. Smith song many times as a teenager. In fact, he won a trophy for singing it at one of those denominational teen talent contests. He later said, had he known how very literally prophetic that song would be, he would have chosen a country hit about living on a million-dollar mountain!

One evening, having been in the CICU for nearly three weeks, Chuck had a sort of freaky, out-of-body thing happen. It was a Sunday night, and I'd stayed later than usual to watch an awards show with him. The fourth wall in that unit is all glass, so it was impossible to miss the scurrying of doctors and nurses that particular night…very uncommon on a Sunday. Before long, word was out that the twenty-year-old girl two doors down was being checked out for a possible match and new heart. I suppose all of that commotion stirred up anxiety in Chuck. Here's how my journal read that next day:

"Well, THAT was a crazy night. What was supposed to be a date night in the CICU became a scary series of events! I think Chuck was nervous, watching all the commotion taking place to prepare Temica

---

[1] Noblitt, Kim. "A New Heart." By Michael W. Smith. Truth. 1980. LP.

for her transplant. At some point in the evening, he started telling me he was going to die. He'd never said anything like that before, and it shook me to the core. I told him he was NOT going to die and not to talk like that. It scared me. Not only did Chuck say it again, in fact, he assured me he was going to die but that I would be OKAY. One time he even pushed me away as he said it. That was just not my Chuck. When he began pacing around the room, the nurses requested a doctor check him out. I called for Barbara to come. His vital signs were fine with the exception of his heart rate being a bit high. Bet mine was too. Dr. Morris was on duty and when he bent over Chuck to check his pupils, Chuck GRABBED him by the collar and quoted the evangelism tool he'd learned years ago, 'If you were to die tonight and stand before God's judgment seat, and if He were to ask you why He should let you into Heaven, what would you say?' Dr. Morris shrugged away from Chuck, straightened his tie sheepishly, and said he did not think his spiritual well-being was important at that moment!! Can't blame a guy for trying, right?"

But in reality, Chuck wasn't acting normal. After checking his vitals, Dr. Morris asked to speak with me in the hall. "If this is some spiritual event Chuck goes through now and again, fine. What do YOU think?"

Me?! I expected HIM to have the answers! Shaking my head, I responded, "I've never met that guy in there!!"

So, off Chuck goes, 2:30 a.m. by now, for a CT Scan to see what might be going on in that head of his. All the way down the hall Chuck sang at the top of his lungs, "I may not sing like the angels…God has given me a new heart!" They got him in the long tube, reminding him to remain still, but within only seconds Chuck would attempt sitting up, smack his head on the machine, and continue singing! Unable to get a scan, Chuck was returned to his room and given a shot of whatever it is they give patients on the psychiatric floor. He slept for two days!

There are names for ICU anxiety attacks…they tend to happen when folks have been there for long periods of time. But this was different. For one thing, he remembered it all and was embarrassed. Try as we did, we never really understood the events of that night, but Chuck felt in his heart that the Lord wanted him to know, He COULD heal that sickly heart in his body like new, but He MIGHT give him a new one instead. Dr. Morris NEVER looked Chuck in the eye again!

Don't We All Need a Heart Transplant?

❧

"My flesh and my heart may fail, but God is the strength
of my heart and my portion forever."

Psalm 73:26

Days became weeks and although Chuck had been moved to the top of the transplant list due to his hospitalization, there are never guarantees of a donor. At one point it appeared he would need an L-VAD, or Left Ventricle Assist Device, implanted, which in those days connected his heart to a large cabinet via wires. The idea was presented to us by doctors with a poster board for visual aid. Upon completion, they revealed, "We've only done this procedure once…on a cow." Chuck, in all of his glory asked if, once finished, they ate their patient! That night I remembered a comment made early on by one of the medical team members that some patients become "toxic" to Lidocaine, the drug keeping his heart numb enough to avoid the quick rhythm that triggered the shocks. They agreed to cut out the drug and he rallied, praise God!

We celebrated Chuck's twenty-eighth birthday in the CICU. Easter, too. We hid eggs and candy in rubber gloves, tissue boxes, and urinals (NEW!). Little Creston was potty trained right there in Room 3402. Six-month-old Nikolai was allowed to visit in spite of the "No one under fourteen years old in the CICU" rule. He was a source of so much joy in the middle of such a stressful time. The staff loved our family, loved our baby boys, and loved Chuck so much! Chuck was the life of the party, even in his weakened state. Still, going to sleep at night was scary for him; it makes sense, but he never mentioned it to me until years later. To keep his mind busy, he borrowed various comedic movies, and one very irreverent VHS tape that had been produced by an ORU TV/Media student. It was clips of a famous evangelist with "toot" sounds edited in! Boy, did that video make Chuck famous! Personnel from all over the hospital came up during the wee hours of the night to watch that three-minute clip! (Can't tell you how badly I'd like to put THAT link in here!!)

My mother came the first week of his hospitalization, and then Barbara came for the duration. We were all tired but took turns between home and the hospital. The following is my journal entry from mid-April 1995:

"It's day thirty-seven. I'm exhausted. I am constantly torn between time with the boys and time with Chuck. I rarely sleep at night between my cluttered-up thoughts and Nikolai's apnea monitor. Seven times last night, God. SEVEN TIMES! Do You even care about us? Seven times I stood over my baby counting — one beep for every second he does not breathe — just waiting for the signal to start CPR. Why is it You prepared me with CPR training? Was it to save my SON or my HUSBAND? I'm glad Chuck is in the hospital. At least he's safe there. But I am fighting...fighting to believe You love us, fighting to believe You will heal Chuck's heart, fighting just to survive each day."

Not one of our more tender conversations, but a real one. There was no time to do a Word study on healing. I had to decide what to believe and then exercise my faith. I'd grown up attending a Presbyterian church. Healing was not a topic that came up much...OKAY, never. But there was a sort of secret meeting held in the old chapel once a month. Praise 'n Prayer it was called, and in that meeting, I'd seen a couple of miracles with my own eyes. I'd seen someone's leg grow out right in the hands of my own dad. I witnessed a shaky man, probably suffering from Parkinson's or MS, become almost completely still, after having seen him many times literally hold his own head still in order to carry on a conversation. Something in me knew it was possible...I just had to figure out if it was probable.

Back when I'd arrived at Oral Roberts University in Tulsa, one of my first questions to the Lord had been, "What *is* Your will about healing?" All my life I'd witnessed my sister's illness and now I was with people who said God always heals, and it's His will to heal. Before I'd learned of His answer, someone prophesied that I'd be used by the Lord in some sort of healing ministry...and now, years later I was facing the need for God's intervention, an opportunity to test it all. In Tulsa, spiritual advice is like air...you can't avoid it and it's often polluted!

"You must believe for healing...God heals EVERYONE."

"My mother died because we weren't dedicated to enough prayer."

"If you just have enough faith...."

And my favorite, "Rebuke the prayers of that Baptist church. They pray for God's will, but are never SPECIFIC enough!!" That just made me shake my head! And, there were many scriptures about Jesus' healing touch in blind eyes, deaf ears, lame people suddenly walking...even the dead raised.

So, I decided God should heal my Chuck...and I made sure everyone knew it. Now THAT'S exercising my faith! As a matter of fact, it's the most exercise Sara had ever experienced in any fashion! My faith was so pumped up and muscular...right up to the last second!

Then, April 19, the Oklahoma City bombing took place. Right down the road...168 lives grievously taken...168 hearts might be available...at least 168 questions raced through my mind. "Do I keep exercising faith if a heart becomes available? Is it showing a lack of faith to receive a transplanted heart instead of waiting on God to heal miraculously?"

Full Moon Over 61st Street

❧

"For I know the plans I have for you," declares the Lord,
"plans to prosper you and not to harm you,
plans to give you hope and a future.
Then you will call on me and come and pray to me,
and I will listen to you. You will seek me and find me
when you seek me with all your heart."

Jeremiah 29:11-13

Being such a glass-half-full kind of guy, Chuck made the most of every day he spent in CICU. During the day we watched TV, listened to music on his boom box, and took time getting to know all of the other patients. Most patients in that unit are not ambulatory…they stay in bed! Not my Chuck! He walked the halls every day, dragging along his IV pole, and soon knew every one of the medical professionals by name. He became the source of comedic stories that to this day are told on that floor! He refused to wear the pink hospital gown, so he was allowed shorts and tank shirts which still provided access for the plethora of tubes and wires.

I spent most every day with him while his mother cared for two-year-old Creston and baby Nikolai. Once dinnertime came, I would leave so that his mom could spend part of the evening there. It was tough leaving him night after night, week after week, but we had a mantra that we said every night, "We're one day closer to this all being over." Then I'd head out and he would wave from the window to make sure I'd made it safely to

47

my car. One night…he turned around, pulled down his shorts…and his SHORTS…and mooned me out the window!! Right there on 61st Street! He had no worries of public nudity charges… it seemed like he was already in jail!

A couple of days after the horrific news of the Oklahoma City bombing, Chuck showed his first and only moments of discouragement. "If 168 lives can be lost just ninety minutes down the road, without a single heart being available…what are my chances?" No one ever wishes death for someone else, but when it happens…and it DOES happen every day…you sure do wish a heroic decision would be made on your behalf. Sunday afternoon, April 23rd, while watching Billy Graham give the Oklahoma City memorial speech, Dr. Ensley came in with two questions. "What are you doing today?" he asked rather nonchalantly "How about a heart transplant?"

You know what's really pitiful? After the doctor walked out, I leaned down over Chuck and whispered, "Maybe it won't match!" Sad, but I had prayed so much for God to heal the heart Chuck already had, I just couldn't believe my faith had not been enough.

There were a number of tests to run to make certain of a match so the TV went off and the activities went into high gear. Forty-some vials of blood were drawn, X-rays taken, nurses rushing in and out…all while we called everyone we knew asking for prayer. Just before heading to surgery, we were patched in to the evening service at our church for a special and very meaningful prayer. Then…hugs, kisses, "see you soon," and he was off, still smiling.

One thing about Chuck…he'd already HAD a heart transplant of sorts…a spiritual one. He'd given his heart…dreams, hopes, wishes…his very life to Jesus many years before. He knew his Redeemer lived and that He had for Chuck a future and a hope. Me? I'd done that too. I knew that too. I had a lot of questions for God, but one thing I knew for sure...I was saved from eternal separation from Him. He was a personal Friend, and that relationship was mine to keep as long as I wanted it. Still, the doctor offered me a Valium!

The Greatest Gift of All

❧

*"Blessed (happy, fortunate, and to be envied) is he who takes no
offense at Me and finds no cause for stumbling in or through Me, and
is not hindered from seeing Truth."*

Matthew 11:6 AMP

After wheeling Chuck into the operating room, his mother and I were taken to wait in a private room near CICU. A handful of friends came to sit and wait with us. I don't remember what Barbara did during those hours…but I spent a good portion of the time arguing with a long-time family friend about a recent report on military hazing. (I was against it!) I'm guessing that Valium worked pretty well! Every twenty to thirty minutes the phone would ring with an update on Chuck's progress.

"His body temp is down."

"We have opened him up and he's doing fine."

"The heart/lung machine is hooked up."

"His heart has been removed." That was a tough call.

But after not much longer we received the final call, "The new heart has been connected and started beating on its own!"

Whew…what a complete sense of relief when *that* news came. In three-and-a-half hours Chuck was back in his room, breathing on his own, though still on the ventilator. By morning he was extubated, sitting up with his new "zipper," and complaining that his feet were too hot... and that "THESE" tear jerker candies were WAAAAY more sour than the other ones he'd been eating. He'd been so long without good circulation, he hadn't realized even his tongue had been compromised. Within just hours Chuck was up walking and putting that new pump to the test.

Sometimes Miracles Hide

❦

"There are only two ways to live your life. One is as though nothing is a miracle. The other is as though everything is a miracle."

Albert Einstein

Still dark outside at 4:30 a.m., I drove home from Saint Francis Hospital half asleep and half restless following the previous night's events. I turned on the radio, hoping it would be the help needed to keep my eyelids open just a few more miles, and a song was playing that I'd never heard before: "Sometimes miracles hide. God will wrap some blessings in disguise. You may wait a lifetime to see with your eyes, 'cause sometimes miracles hide." I wondered if God put that song on the radio just for me. Maybe He even wrote it…I'd never heard it before, and I've never heard it since…but what God had allowed the night before had completely overruled the huge faith I had risked, and I needed to hear a miracle was still a possibility. I needed to know God had a plan that would reach beyond what I could see. I needed to remember "Many are the plans in a person's heart, but it is the Lord's purpose that prevails" (Proverbs 19:21).

In only nine days we brought our Chuck home…well, only nine days after fifty-some days. During the time he was hospitalized, people were very good to us. My house was cleaned, meals were prepared, and the boys were watched and loved on. So even though my head was spinning with questions, I wanted to remember the good things God did both through His flock at Christian Chapel and through medicine. Barbara once said the biggest miracle of all was that she had survived living seven weeks with her "northern daughter-in-law"! We stretched each other, mostly in good ways!

First stop after getting Chuck settled into his long-awaited shower was to pick up his list of prescriptions from Walgreens. Thankfully, for a while we still had the $5 co-pay which came to $85. The tech handed me two large brown sacks full of meds and with a look of amazement whispered the retail price, "This comes to $5,000+ per month!" No wonder we got personal Christmas cards from the pharmacist!

Over the next days and weeks we received numerous calls and visitors…usually with meals in hand. One after another would hug us, their faces full of delight with all that had taken place…and then they'd say something like, "Isn't it a miracle?!?"

With gritted teeth and half a smile I'd agree, "Yeah…," but the truth was, to me a miracle would have been supernatural healing. To me a miracle would have been God revealing Himself to that self-righteous doctor. To me medicine healed Chuck. God had just let down one of His biggest lifetime fans. I was about to fulfill that scripture in reverse, because if those who take NO offense at Him, and find NO cause for stumbling in OR through Him, and are NOT hindered from seeing His Truth are "blessed (happy, fortunate, and to be envied)"…then I was definitely NOT going to be blessed, happy, fortunate, or envied. I. Was. Angry.

Your Turn

Do you know for certain that you have received a spiritual heart transplant? Jot down the date and the circumstances if you remember! (For the record, I do NOT know my date because I was only seven...but I do remember B. J. Thomas was speaking at the event! Probably sang about Raindrops!)

_____

_____

_____

_____

_____

_____

_____

_____

_____

_____

_____

If you are NOT certain about the condition of your heart, it's as simple as saying something like this:

"Jesus, I've made poor choices for which I ask forgiveness. From today onward, I'm inviting You to lead my life, be my Lord, Savior, and Friend."

Today YOU have undergone a spiritual heart transplant!! Congratulations, Friend! Welcome to the family of God!!

A Song of Lost Hope

His Gifts Are Without Reproach

"Ah, music,' he said, wiping his eyes.
'A magic beyond all we do here!'"

J. K. Rowling

Music was a big part of growing up in the Rinehart family. Both of my parents sang with beautiful voices, often carrying solos in the church choir or singing for weddings and funerals. "He Touched Me... and ma-a-ade me whole!" I remember that Gaither song well. My older sisters all participated in music one way or another. Sue was my soon-to-become-a-famous-singer sister that I wanted to be someday, Ann played flute, and Jane sang in a rock band called TEZE! I thought that was so cool! I was torn between becoming Olivia Newton-John...and violinist, Itzhak Perlman! Whenever company was over, we knew a concert would soon commence!

One particular autumn, I found myself truly broken over the condition of the hearts of some of my favorite musicians. I had never owned a Barry Manilow record...but felt completely burdened for his soul. I had been given the opportunity to sing backup in his Denver concert one year (in a group!), and I saw such great talent...and such emptiness in his eyes. Among others, the lives of my Russian violin teacher and my school choir director, Ms. Adams, consumed my mind day and night. "Their gifts were created to honor God...they just don't know Him yet. They play and sing

59

with anointing (yes, God's gifts are without reproach - Romans 11:29), but right now the glory goes only to themselves."

After building up that courage to be vulnerable, I confided in my sister Jane. She suggested perhaps God was allowing me to feel the grief He feels for those whom He's created, and gifted…those who are lost. (Yes, we Christians call you who don't know Him YET, "lost"!) I remembered then a quote I'd heard by the founder of World Vision, "Let my heart be broken with the things that break Yours." Maybe that was it…maybe I was just sampling the immeasurable grief of God as He watches His precious creations live apart from His grace and love…apart from His provision and direction. To think He felt a grief so much deeper than I could even fathom…terrible.

Back to 1995. With Chuck gaining strength and life becoming more normal, we began accepting invitations to speak and sing in local churches. Chuck would share his story with all of the hilarity that so easily came to him…and I would knock everyone down with the sobering truth…God is sovereign. With transparency, I shared about my anger at God and the fact that my faith did not seem to matter to Him…He did what He wanted anyway. I described my mind's picture of Jesus, brown-eyed, tenderhearted, warm and loving…and of God, blue-eyed, stern, and far off; and how I'd only recently been able to picture the Holy Spirit. I shared about a sermon that had aided in my heart's understanding. Our pastor had described the Holy Spirit as simply a Friend. He is the One who goes to the Father with "groans" we cannot ourselves even voice (Romans 8:26-27). THAT was the answer…when I had refused to pray in advance for the donor family who would lose someone they loved, when I had prayed with all my arrogant pride and TOLD the Lord that I was not interested in His will if it included transplantation…my lifelong Friend, the Holy Spirit, was going to God on my behalf. "Father, she's crazy right now! Sara cannot see beyond her exhaustion. Let's look instead at her past character…remember her as one who DOES seek Your face…when she's sane!!" Isn't that what a friend would do? Those words moved the people in our services. That kind of Truth spoke volumes to the broken hearts filling the seats before us.

Ephesians 3:18 says, "I pray that you, the SAINTS, will understand how high, how deep, how long, and how wide is the love of God…" (Saraphrased). Isn't it strange how Paul was saying that to the Christians? Shouldn't THEY be the ones who already *know* how high, deep, long, and wide God's love is? But in reality…it was the saints in Bible times and it is the saints still today, the Christians, the pastors, and church leaders who, over and over, came to us following our services, weeping, broken, and disappointed in God and without anyone in whom to confide. Perhaps even YOU relate? My heart broke for these people JUST like it had for those musicians who were special to me as a teenager, and I wanted nothing more than for them to realize how very much God loved them and wanted only good for them. Sundays, Wednesdays, whenever the invitation was there, we spoke and sang and prayed for the love of God to overwhelm those in attendance. The only problem was…I didn't believe it was true for myself.

Is God Stingy?

❧

"I need to know the Truth, and I need something I can feel.
I need You to make it real."

Suzanne Jennings

Five years after Chuck received his new heart, we were blessed with Asher Gracen, another little boy. We thought and prayed about that decision for quite some time, and had even asked good ol' Dr. Ensley if there were any risks in having another child. Chuck took a colorful array of medicines to prevent rejection, and another collection of vitamins and minerals to make up for what the anti-rejection meds depleted. Dr. E's typical no-bedside-manner response was, "You'd better consider the life expectancy of the father." We weren't completely taken aback by that response! Chuck bit his tongue that day, keeping back the words, "You might get hit by a car TODAY…we never know, do we?!"

The Lord gave us a peace about continuing our family, but still, the broken truster in me suggested I'd probably miscarry so God could use me to minister to the women who have lost babies. Every time I began to trust a little, I'd assume the worst would happen so I could be used by God. I had lost the glass-half-full girl I once was. James McDonald said in his book, *Christ-Centered Biblical Counseling,* "Satan mounts his mutiny against God through a deceitful stronghold: God is untrustworthy. In subtle and not-so-subtle ways, he places God's heart on trial by whispering lies: 'God is holding back on you. He wants you to jump through hoops in order to earn His love. He's stingy. He doesn't have your best interest in mind. You're better off trusting in yourself. Your resources and functional saviors work better than waiting and trusting in Him.'" UGH! The enemy is such a liar! Ephesians 1:7-8 says that because of Jesus' sacrifice, we're FREE people, and not just barely free, but abundantly free! He's NOT stingy, but in fact, richly blesses all who call on Him (Romans 10:12).

There are many stories and events from those first several years which drew me closer to the Savior I'd always known, but also a few things that caused me to step back and rethink that faith thing again. I did learn one big lesson. God was and is always at work to woo His creations to His heart. If you are one who is feeling like God has turned His back, or that He has been stingy, consider rethinking that today. I believe He is right there in the muck with you…face-to-Face…broken heart to Broken Heart…ready to intervene at the perfect time. Suzanne Jennings wrote a song that speaks to this very feeling of needing something tangible to help us through those times when the world's darkness has blinded us to Him.

Maybe you can relate.

Make It Real

(by Suzanne Jennings)

I've seen a lot of crazy things done in your name
I know the tricks behind the magic show
I've almost thrown the towel in a time or two
And walked away from everything I know
But I can't fill the emptiness inside of me
Or calm the troubled waters of my mind
So if you're really out there and you're listening
Then prove to me that those who seek will find
If you can just see fit to show me some of who you are

If you can shed some light into this broken sinner's heart
I need to know the truth
And I need something I can feel
I need you to make it real
There must be some good reason
Why you brought me here
Through valleys where the shadows hover close
'cause down here there's a mask to cover every face
But your sweet face I long to see the most
So if you think there's just the slightest hope for me
In spite of all my questions and my doubts
Then let me hear your still, small voice
Speak out my name
And let me know what others talk about
If you can just see fit to show me some of who you are
If you can shed some light into this broken sinner's heart
I need to know the truth
And I need something I can feel
I need you to make it real
Lord, I need to know the truth
And I need something I can feel
I need you – please, make it real [2]

All of us need that assurance at some time in our lives. Even the disciple Thomas, who walked with Jesus on a daily basis, seeing miracles firsthand, doubted His resurrection until he saw Jesus face-to-face. Having seen Him crucified, I would likely have doubted too, wouldn't you? God gets it. Ask Him to make it real for you too.

---

[2] Lowry, Mark. "Make it Real," by Suzanne Jennings. Mark Lowry Goes To Hollywood. 2005. CD.

My Truster Broke

❧

"Trust in the Lord with all your heart, and
LEAN NOT ON YOUR OWN UNDERSTANDING;
in all your ways acknowledge Him, and He shall direct your path."
Proverbs 3:5-6 NKJV (emphasis mine)

Damen Ballard, twenty-five, left his apartment April 19, 1995, to grab a pack of cigarettes at the convenience store. On his way back he took the shortcut…crossing I-44 on foot at rush hour. He was hit and became a John Doe while doctors tried to save his life. Even as we were watching the terrible news of the Oklahoma City bombing down the road…and fighting against all of those feelings of desperation when we discovered no hearts would be coming…Chuck's new heart was just two floors above us in the very same hospital.

In time, we were allowed to correspond with the family of Chuck's donor. We met Damen's parents at a little hole-in-the-wall diner between our home and theirs. Anna, being American Indian, knew that organ donation was not a custom her ancestors practiced, but she believed Damen was communicating with her still, and even called our little Asher her "Heart Grandson." One morning, while singing in Arkansas, that sweet little couple came on stage so we could introduce them as the selfless parents who gave so that Chuck could live…Anna laid her head on Chuck's chest to hear the beat of her son's heart. Not a dry eye in the place!

Chuck and I continued traveling to minister, sing, speak and pray over brokenhearted Christians who were confused and hurt by the church and even by their understanding of God. I continued too, sympathizing with them and broken for them. But off stage, I was one of them. When communion elements were passed down my row Sunday morning, I left them under my chair. I could not commune with a God who did not honor my bigger-than-mustard-seed faith. I was more than certain God loved people…but I was also nearly certain He just needed *me* as a tool of transparency. My truster was broken. Having loved God my whole life, I couldn't think of anything better…anywhere else to turn…so I just kept on serving and assuming the love and peace of God were for everyone but me. I didn't read His Word unless it was a story for one of my little guys. I didn't pray unless it was a mommy or wife kind of prayer. My only hope for healing was the remnant of verses I had hidden away in my heart over the years. Would God's Word be alive and relevant enough to draw me back to Him? Deep down, I thought it might…I hoped it would…someday.

Never Left or Forsaken

✧

"Lo, I am with you always, even unto the end of the world."

Matthew 28:20 KJV

The Bible, in the book of Matthew, recounts the story of the crucifixion of Jesus. As He died, He said the words, "My God, My God, why have You forsaken Me?" (Matthew 27:46 NKJV). If you are one who attends church regularly (or perhaps just at Christmas and Easter), you've likely heard someone say God turned His back on Jesus...that the sin upon Jesus was so great, God could no longer look at Him. I'm no Bible scholar, but I choose to interpret that differently. Deuteronomy 31:6 says, "Be strong and courageous. Do not be terrified for the Lord your God goes with you; he will NEVER leave you nor forsake you" (emphasis mine).

What if Jesus, while clouded with the sin of the whole world and covered with the stripes of every disease, just could not FEEL His Father's presence? What if God was there all along, grieving while watching the unrelenting beating, mocking, and torture of His Son? Why would God leave Jesus at His greatest point of desperation when He says He will NEVER leave us nor forsake us? I don't think He did or He does, though sometimes it sure FEELS like He's gone.

As it often happens, my relationship with God has grown and developed over the years. The first seven years following Chuck's heart transplant were mostly days of frustration and anger at Him. BUT, there were days here and there that God's love for me sneaked in and I'd give Him a smile from my heart...a sort of "I know You're there...I'll probably be back... but You've got some proving to do!" If that sounds very irreverent and disrespectful to you...you're right...but that's how He and I do this life together! I gripe and moan, He rolls His eyes...I ask for forgiveness, then we restore! It's a daily process! For some of us, it's moment by moment.

One evening a few years after my truster broke, Chuck and I had a fancy New Year's event at which to sing and speak. By then I was testing the Lord's love with little prayers, always careful not to get TOO hopeful in the event that SOVEREIGNTY got in the way. I knelt down by my bed that morning, and told the Lord I had nothing fancy to wear and no money to buy anything. I asked Him to provide something sparkly for the evening's event. I think I was praying and brainstorming at the same time...wondering who might have something I could borrow. In the mail that afternoon I received a box from Denver...a friend of my mom's had decided she no longer had need of a sequined sweater and thought maybe I could use it in my singing!

All these years later, that is one of the most loved-by-God moments in my life. He cared enough to help me feel pretty. He'd arranged, days in advance, for someone to go through her closet, box up a sweater, head to the post office, and mail me just what I needed the very night it would arrive. That sweater was a source of healing. The beginning of a realization was taking place. Sovereignty and faith DO work together; it happens as relationship with God deepens.

By the Blood of the Lamb

⚜

"Never be bitter, become better.
A testimony is pain that has been reassigned."

Johnnie Dent Jr.

My journals are full of entries diametrically opposing each other. Praising God one day and the next telling Him, "I sure appreciate that parking ticket YOU allowed while we were waiting on a doctor to see our HEARING IMPAIRED son!" (Sweet Nikolai, though he'd never displayed delays in speech or learning, was diagnosed at eight years old as profoundly deaf!) One day I'd write thanking Him for providing for another bill, and the next telling Him He's mean for allowing my Creston to become diabetic, especially as I'd lost a sister to that terrible disease. One day I'd be high as a kite about an answer to prayer, and the next I'd remind God that this last kiddo He gave me has a brain that works in a manner opposite of mine...so He BETTER help me raise him! Still, my broken truster was in the process of repair.

It took a long time and a LOT of God showing Himself faithful. Things that we could not have done for ourselves, like a couple of opportunities to sing and speak with the Billy Graham Association (seventeen minutes and not a second longer!) and a job as National Directors of Couples Ministry with Stonecroft Ministries, were faith builders...only God could have orchestrated those events. They came at times we were at the end of ourselves. Doesn't that seem to be His way? At the end of me there's Him.

At the end of doing it MY way…there's HIS way. Those jobs gave me hope that He was IN this life He had ALLOWED.

One day a friend of ours, who has suffered very difficult times in her own life, asked me how I got over my anger towards God. I really didn't know. I told her I'd get back to her and prayed like crazy for the next few days. The answer seemed so simple…the Lord took me to Revelation 12:11 NKJV: "They overcame him (the accuser of the brethren in the verse before) by the blood of the Lamb and by the word of their testimony…." Seven plus years of telling my story, over and over and over…and seven plus years of hearing Chuck's amazing rendition of his side of the story, both sprinkled with scripture and laughter, had been a healing balm to my broken truster…even when I didn't believe it to be truth for me. God's Word is not supposed to return void…empty…and it did not. Along with that, time with my Heavenly Father, the deepening of that relationship, was automatically causing my heart to desire what His heart desires. And with the events that were to come…a whole and working truster was going to be necessary.

I encourage you to look back over your story. Spend a little time remembering the good things; take just a moment to touch on the times of trial. Write down how you feel, what you've seen God do or NOT do. You just might see a common thread working throughout your life. It could begin the process of your restoration and deepen your heart for God. Your tapestry is in the works.

Your Turn

Have you ever felt as though God has been stingy? In what shape is YOUR truster? Whole and working? Broken? Cracked, but intact? Ask the Lord to help you trust Him. If you've never given Him a chance...step out! It's OKAY...ask Him to make it real for you today!

_____

_____

_____

_____

_____

_____

_____

_____

_____

_____

_____

_____

_____

Songs of Faith

Laughter Doeth Good

❧

"There are times when you wish the commode had a seat belt…"[3]

Dave Barry

There are a lot of ups and downs that come with organ transplantation. Every week for a while, then every month, and eventually out to a year, Chuck had heart biopsies. He'd watch the little Pac-Man looking thing on the screen as it yanked out eight to ten pieces of his heart! One word to which we held tightly was "adopt." Our dear Pastor Davis had visited and prayed with Chuck every morning in the hospital at about 6:30…every morning! The morning following surgery he prayed that Chuck's heart would be adopted by his body as its own. He wouldn't have known, but that day was the anniversary of Chuck's being adopted by his forever family twenty-eight years before. What a sweet confirmation from the Lord.

Chuck was all about proving he could keep up with the other guys his age, and once medically released, he had permission to do anything except skydive! So he never went skydiving, but we did go rappelling…and once he tried a tree swing along with a bunch of church men only to get caught up on a nail. He ended up hanging over rocks like a hammock, all the guys laughing hysterically, only able to reach his rear by their fingertips for support! With muscles atrophied from months of being in bed, he ended

---

[3] Miami Herald, 22 February 2008.

up falling and tearing cartilage in his rib cage, which then caused big rejection. Lesson learned.

But, it seemed like at just the right time, when we needed a good hard laugh, there'd be something to fulfill that need. Twice during his post-transplant years, Chuck experienced some rhythm issues with the beat of his new heart. The first time he chose to (as Dr. Ensley put it) "have a meeting with the electric company" in order to shock it back into the normal sinus rhythm. Thirty seconds of amnesia medicine, one "CLEAR," one big shock…and he was set to go home!

The second time, the problem was due to an overabundance of potassium in his system. He was prescribed a medicine which could be taken orally OR rectally! He chose the oral route! That night, I was awakened by a huge explosion…I mean the kind of explosion you hear from a newborn baby, but louder!! Bless his heart, determined to never be cold again, Chuck was sleeping in socks and long johns…shirt tucked in neatly! He flew out of bed and into the bathroom. I lie quietly…not wanting to embarrass him! Nearly an hour later, and following a shower, he emerged with lights out. Unable to resist the opportunity, I asked him if everything was okay. Standing stark naked, holding a plastic bag filled with long johns unfit for anything except burning, he flipped on the light…"Does this answer your question?!!?" He described the whole process of disrobing from items covered in…you know what…over his head, no less!! No exaggeration, I laughed for three hours! Every time I'd settle back down, that explosive noise came to mind and the bed would begin shaking as I tried to keep quiet!! Laughter was indeed good medicine!

Disability Disables

❧

*"Government, even in its best state, is but a necessary evil;
in its worst state, an intolerable one."*

Thomas Paine

For about ten years, neither Chuck nor I had a real job. I know?! Can you imagine? Chuck had been placed on Social Security Disability shortly after receiving the new heart. The laws at the time were very strict and very limiting to both Chuck and me. He was not allowed to work at all, and I was limited in what I could make. I'll never forget the letter we received saying I'd made too much money (working in the church nursery twice a week!). Consequently, they would reduce what we were receiving from Disability. What?? I am not disabled!! Why can't I work?!

It was a vicious cycle. We (I) would earn enough to help make ends meet...they'd reduce what we received. At one point my own parents suggested I divorce Chuck quietly. Nothing would change, but I'd be allowed to work and take care of expenses. I knew it was just a passing comment... more of a shot at the lame government...but it felt like a bullet in my heart. The burden of responsibility I felt was unbearable at times. Our singing helped with living expenses, of course, and it was worked out legally by a CPA so that we did not break any laws. Still, it was feast or famine. When we had a good month with a lot of singing, every cent went to car repairs, new tires, or things for the boys that had been on the back burner. By the tenth year, I had all but fallen apart. Something had to change. We felt a willingness to step forward...but could see no doors or even windows through which to go.

The Church Is Not a Building

⸎

"A ship is always safe at the shore,
but that's not what ships are built for!"

Albert Einstein

Change seemed to be in the air. In January of 2003 we began feeling a stirring in our hearts about leaving our church. As happens, our church was going through a time of change and growth; however, as far ahead as we could plan, our boys would be finding wives there, getting married there, and growing our grandchildren there! One particular Sunday afternoon, after having grown and learned and served at Christian Chapel for fifteen years, Chuck and I found ourselves sick to our stomachs that we had both heard from the Lord that morning..."You are released from Christian Chapel. Today was your last day." No warning. No church shopping around for a few months. That was our last day.

We began the horrible task of looking for a new church home. Don't do it if you don't have to! I cried every Sunday! People were not friendly, they did not welcome us. More than once I stood in a foyer with my three boys...inquisitive expression on my face, wondering where children's ministry was...and more than once, nobody offered to help. With my parents having recently moved to Tulsa, we all decided to settle down at Asbury United Methodist Church. There, we were welcomed, received a personal phone call by the pastor, and our boys had places to hear about Jesus. It was not long before we were singing with the worship team, and had fostered a new friendship which led us to our first big opportunity to test out the scripture…"And my God shall supply all your needs according to the riches of his glory in Christ Jesus" (Philippians 4:19).

Through a contact from a member of the worship team, Chuck was offered that position I mentioned earlier with Stonecroft Ministries as the National Director of Couples Ministry. There was a lot of risk in taking that job as the laws at the time stated a person could not reapply for Disability benefits for the same problem twice. That meaning, if Chuck found himself unable to keep up with full-time job responsibilities after giving it a try…we were SOL (Shoot out of Luck!). The excitement for change made it all worth the risk!! We took it!

Stonecroft was celebrating their seventieth year of ministry to women. So, starting a new chapter including couples was really exciting and a bit scary! Chuck and I were flown all over the country to speak and sing. We collaborated with a wonderful dramatic teacher friend, Dawn, who helped us put together a "Drama-mony"…Chuck would tell his story in real time and with humor, and I would play myself, writing in my journal, that which came to mind in those very troubling times. It proved to be very effective and so many people came to know Jesus through the creative rendition of His faithfulness, even in our weaknesses. We were humbled and honored to have that great opportunity to travel and speak. And God provided in gracious ways so that we could homeschool the boys along the way. With Chuck being the upbeat, promoter guy he was, Stonecroft often called upon him to participate in the development weekends when they "wined and dined" guests who might be able to help further God's Kingdom with their financial help.

After a number of years, Stonecroft and their new CEO made the decision to discontinue the Couples Ministry position. Honestly, we had begun to suspect change was coming, and were relieved we were not asked to relocate to the Headquarters in Kansas City!

———

Fall of 2006, we had enrolled our boys at Augustine Christian Academy (ACA), a private school with an emphasis in classical education. I had home educated all of them up until that point, so our "First Day of School" picture was all three of them, long dress pants, ties, and the older boys wearing suit coats! Stonecroft had paid us well…what a wonderful feeling it had been to pay all of our bills and have something left with which to meet random needs or even some wants! ACA provided some financial aid for us, and Chuck offered to write grants for them, seeking help from someone he'd met in the Toastmasters organization. That contact made way for his offer to work full time, writing grants for Oral Roberts University…and THAT provided free college education for my boys! I guess God really does open the storehouses and pour out blessings when we obey! The risk and the pain of change…God had made all things new. More healing was taking place in my truster with each new day.

Non-Hodgkin's Lymphoma

❧

"With every breath, with every thought, from what is seen to the deepest part, I offer all that I've come to be, to know Your love fathering me. Father, You're all I need, my soul's sufficiency, my strength when I am weak, that love that carries me. Your arms enfold me, till I am only a child of God."

Kathryn Scott[4]

Those lyrics began my blog January 1, 2011…a blog I hoped would be a new sort of journal – maybe just for me, or maybe a journal I'd share publicly. It was a blog that never saw another post. I suppose it's out there in cyberspace somewhere. I've forgotten under what title it is, or even what my password might have been. What I DO remember are the tears that ran down my cheeks that day as I typed out that song, and the prayer that followed. Somewhere deep inside I knew rough days were ahead. I remember wondering if God was preparing me for the coming trial…or if the enemy was just filling my head with nonsense.

In a few days, my Chuck would undergo a biopsy on three small lumps he had discovered in his neck before Christmastime. Maybe they were a result of swollen glands from the common winter cold…or maybe… more likely…they were a symptom of a disease the name of which I could not bring myself to voice. A sense that something was coming that would challenge our hearts was clear; but knowing grace would be sufficient to

---

[4] Scott, Kathryn. "Child of God." Vineyard Songs, 1999.

withstand it seemed somehow just as clear that day. It didn't mean I wasn't afraid…it didn't stop the tears that New Year's morning. It just left me with an assurance that God would not let us go. That kind of trust was a long time in coming. John 10:29 reminded me, no *one* or no *thing* is able to snatch us from the Father's hand. No one or no thing is able to snatch you from His hand either, Friend.

A few days later the diagnosis came: Non-Hodgkin's Lymphoma.

I give myself unreservedly
To know Your love fathering me.
Father, You're all I need,
My soul's sufficiency,
My strength when I am weak,
The love that carries me.
Your arms enfold me, till I am only,
A Child of God.[5]

---

[5] Scott, Kathryn. "Child of God." Vineyard Music, 1999.

It'll Take Rocket Fuel

❧

"We can make our plans, but the Lord determines our steps."

Proverbs 16:9 NLT

Chuck's insurance referred us to an oncologist named Dr. Strnad, (Chuck met him and asked, "May I buy a vowel?"!) We "auditioned" him with the arms of our hearts crossed in a "prove yourself" sort of way. First impressions can be so deceiving! He walked in wearing jeans, cowboy boots, and sporting a long, salt-and-pepper ponytail...but within just a few moments we both knew he was the man for the job. It was supposed to be so easy, I mean for cancer. Having caught it early, only six chemo treatments were prescribed. A little hair loss...a few sickly days...and BOOM...cancer free! Six rough months...that's it!

We set up a group on Facebook and called it "Chuck's Butt Kicking Friends," That would be his way of keeping all of our friends from all over the country and the world, up to date on his progress of kicking cancer's butt. His forty-fourth birthday was just around the corner, so we decided to have a big party a few days before with any and all of the Butt Kicking Friends who could attend. Chuck had T-shirts printed that read, "Kick Ask (on Cancer) and You Shall Receive!" People bought them at the party to help with the upcoming expenses. I'd ordered a cake at the local bakery, but they refused to put "Kick Ask" on it...they wouldn't even put the words "Kick Butt"! Hilarious! You'd have thought I was requesting two grooms atop it! There was a hat/wig contest that night, a sort of get-ready-to-be-bald theme! We wrapped up the night singing worship led by Chuck. Great birthday party!

On March 15, 2011, Chuck had spent the evening of his *actual* forty-fourth birthday leading worship at a Celebrate Recovery meeting. He came home feeling a little under the weather and was sure it was the mushrooms from lunch out. Whatever it was…he was sick all night…and all of the next day. I kept liquids by the bed, took his temp, and passed out Tylenol, but mostly let him rest. By mid-afternoon, Asher and I decided to make a run for a new game…a little spring break adventure. While away, Chuck called, barely audible saying he needed to go to the hospital. Within forty-five minutes, he was on his way…via ambulance.

Treatment #1 had gone well. No vomiting, no weakness, no issues at all…the first week. But, being immune-suppressed makes fighting disease tricky; suddenly we found ourselves in critical shape.

"Hey, all Chuck's Facebook friends, Chuck is in CICU and is fighting for his life. Please pray!! He needs a miracle." – Carol

So much for easy. The above was one of the first posts in the "Chuck's Butt Kicking Friends" Facebook group. We never expected that it would be such a means for our desperate cries for prayer.

When an organ is transplanted into a new body, it is often rejected by that very system it was placed there to save. It's how God made us to heal ourselves. We fight things foreign to our system. That is what makes transplantation difficult; finding the balance in medicine so the body can fight viruses without fighting the new organ. So, as the chemo began its toll on Chuck's body, he was unable to fight off common, daily germs that were likely in his system long before chemo began. He became septic in a matter of hours. THAT causes organ failure, and THAT causes death.

With every minute in that ER, breathing became more difficult. His blood pressure plummeted to 60/30, and I was not about to let another minute go by without a doctor who knew my Chuck! Years of patient advocating made it almost natural to take matters into my own hands; I called the head of heart transplantation from right there in the ER, and Dr. Ensley came down immediately. I remember him looking into Chuck's eyes and asking him, "Am I President Obama?" Chuck's eyebrows furrowed, and he shook his head, "No." He still had a little sense left in him! Hours later and after getting Chuck semi-stable, Dr. Ensley took Creston and me to a private waiting area where he very graciously told us we needed to call in the family. The chances of living through the night were less than fifty percent. Funny, that was the first time I'd seen a tender side of Dr. E. In spite of the shocking and dreadful news he'd just given me, I wanted to hug him for being there for my Chuck and me all over again.

Behind the scenes, God was already at work. During the hours Chuck was being stabilized in the ER, the head nurse over nine floors was busy getting rooms and beds for all of the new patients. With one bed left in the Cardiac ICU, she began preparations for an 18-year-old woman; however, the Spirit of God spoke to her heart, and she called the ER to see if anyone with significant heart issues might need the room instead. She was told there was, in fact, a heart transplant recipient needing a room and then was given five minutes to have it ready for Chuck Stophel. She told us days later that her own heart skipped a beat when she heard his name…we attended church together! Had she not listened to the Holy Spirit, Chuck would not have been able to be under the direct care of Dr. Ensley, the only doctor who knew his whole history. I don't believe Chuck would have lived through the night without the very aggressive actions he prescribed. We were told a number of times by various specialists, "Chuck is the sickest patient in this hospital." God knew who needed to be there for Chuck!

The chances of living through the night were small, and nobody beat around the bush about it. Infection had reached his blood stream. He was intubated, and being "rocket fueled" with lines and lines of life-supporting drugs. Creston (18), Nikolai (16), and I walked into Chuck's room to express our love, pour out prayers, and cling to hope that God in His sovereignty had more days ahead for our hero. Asher (10) stood at the foot of the bed for a moment. Overcome by emotion, he ran away in tears.

The Body of Christ

❧

"How beautiful on the mountains are the feet of the messenger
bringing good news, breaking the news that all's well, proclaiming
good times, announcing salvation, telling Zion, 'Your God reigns!'"

Isaiah 52:7 MSG

The CICU waiting room was full that night, to the point of overflowing into the halls. Praying for us, singing hymns on our behalf…just gathering to meet any needs were pastors and friends from several churches where we had either attended or spoken. Dozens of teens from the boys' school came and stayed until the wee hours of the night.

There was nothing they could do…but they meant the world to the boys and me. Actually, I saw Jesus that night. I mean it. I saw Him many times over the following weeks. He came in the form of Chuck's dear friend Stan, taking his vacation days just to BE there when needed. He came with crackers and ice cold drinks in a cooler. He came with Hospital Survival Kits full of silly games, funny movies, and snacks. He brought a prayer shawl, lovingly crocheted with a prayer in every stitch. He appeared as a beautiful Filipino woman bearing Rosary beads which had been blessed by the Pope himself! He came with a candle that was lit in a Jewish Temple on our behalf. I knew there was no power in those beads or in that candle… but the faith of those who did believe moved mountains in our hearts. Those people are the Body of Christ. His hands, His feet, His voice, and His Words spoken over us…He was there. Prayers were lifted up from nations literally around the world…even a little note of prayer placed in the Wailing Wall on behalf of my Chuck.

Chuck's Facebook page was growing in numbers with people we'd never met before. We fondly gave the members the name, "Butt Kickers"! A few samples of the early posts follow:

"Been bedside with Dad all night. He can respond via squeezing our hands or an occasional eyebrow lift." – Creston

"Dad has been given multiple bags of fluids with very little output meaning his kidneys are not working. Please pray that he starts peeing! (as blunt as that may be, have fun with it, God gave us humor!)" – Creston

"Thank you for your continued prayers. Chuck's heart is said to be his healthiest organ!" – Kathryn

"I'm a night owl, so lifting your family up in prayers right now!" – Valerie

"Between the cardiologist, oncologist, nephrologist (kidney doc), internist, and the hospitalist…they cannot grow a bug. For now they are treating for every kind of infection until they figure out what he really needs!" – Sara

It was heartbreaking to see his hands tied down, and yet we knew that signs of fighting the tubes meant he still had fight in him. He suffered temporary kidney failure as a result of the sepsis…and one of my MOST favorite Facebook posts was from a gal in Texas who said she had sixteen women praying for a man they do not know but were beginning to love… to PEE!!

With eager anticipation, we'd await Dr. Ensley's morning report of the blood work (taken at 4:00 a.m.). Every morning he would say Chuck was a little better…and then add, "We're still a MILLION miles away!" But after seventeen years of Dr. E, I had developed the gift of interpretation… that was good news!

So here I was. Another opportunity to pray for healing. Another opportunity for God to move a mountain. An opportunity to figure out if faith includes submission to sovereignty. I was committed to praying for healing for more years for my husband. I was committed to stand, hope, and believe for God to move in his body mightily…all while being careful to guard my heart and my truster. "My flesh and my heart may fail, but God is the strength of my heart and my portion forever" (Psalm 73:26).

───────

Advocating for a patient takes a mixed bag of tricks. I had to be sweet enough to be liked and respected, but tough enough to show I understood what was going on and had expectations for my husband's care. One doctor would prescribe medicine to sedate Chuck so he would relax. Another would prescribe a Sedation Vacation (removing all sedation) to see if he was strong enough to be taken off the vent. One doctor would prescribe dialysis to get him off the vent with more ease. Another would say dialysis was too taxing on a body and weaning would have to wait. At some point I had to bring out the redheaded Sara O'Stophel…the Irish in me! Never be afraid to advocate! We had an all-hands-on-deck kind of meeting, and came up with a plan to get Chuck off the ventilator and on the road to recovery! It worked!

By day eight, Chuck woke up enough to desire communication, but without the capability to do it. His fingers were not limber enough to use good ol' American Sign Language spelling so we tried an alphabet board at which he could gaze. I tried my best to hide my frustration, but I had no idea what "FKAGBR" meant, and he desperately wanted me to get it!

Nine days and nights, Creston spent nearly every moment at the foot of Chuck's bed. Nikolai kept the visitors feeling welcomed down in "our" waiting room. He kept them abreast of the latest news…and kept me from having to do it myself. Facebook was blasted with loving comments about how beautifully our boys had walked out their faith and courage during the most difficult of times, in front of both believers and nonbelievers. I could not have been more proud of them all. My biggest concern after Chuck had been Asher…but the Lord graciously provided him with families to entertain him and keep his mind occupied.

When Chuck was finally extubated and awake…he had NO memory of the past nine days…and no idea what his parents were doing in Tulsa! Oh…so much to explain….

Mr. Facebook Man

"And who knows but that you have come to the kingdom
for such a time as this and for this very occasion?"

Esther 4:14 AMP

Social media was a lifesaver for me. As is often God's way, opposites DO attract. Chuck was charged up by people; the more people, the more fun and energy he had! Bless his heart, I am, in fact, the opposite! No offense intended here, but people exhaust me! That's part of what made us such a great match, we were well-balanced on our social calendar! Because of that, Facebook was a wonderful gift as I was able to keep literally thousands of people from all over the world informed daily about Chuck's condition... and I did not have to say it over and over in person.

This is a letter I wrote to Mark Zuckerberg, the founder of Facebook. I imagine he'll never actually READ it, but I needed to say it just in case.

Dear Mr. Facebook Man,

I want to share with you a story about...you. March 16th this year, my husband became very ill and was taken via ambulance to the hospital. Infection had overtaken his body, he was in septic shock and within hours I was told to bring in our three boys to say good-bye to their dad. Creston-eighteen, Nikolai-sixteen, and Asher-ten stood at the foot of his bed and expressed their love through tears. My husband never knew it. Chuck had been intubated and was in an induced coma.

Across the hospital, my friends activated Facebook requesting prayer for Chuck, and very shortly there were people all over the country…the world, praying for him! We believed that the God who made him could fix him now! He improved. Messages began flowing in from Norway and Israel, Honduras and nearly all fifty states! He improved. People were praying from their Christian faith, their Jewish faith, some who have NO faith but just love Chuck! He improved! Day and night, night and day…prayers have been raised; specific prayers for specific needs. He improved more!

So, how is this a story about YOU? Because I believe you were gifted by the God who created you for such a time as this. You may have had other intentions for your social media program, but God knew a much bigger picture. You thought it was a great moneymaker (and it was)… but God knew it would connect people all over the world just when we needed it. You thought high school friends would reconnect, but God knew that we could share specific needs for specific prayers…and He would show His faithfulness. God knew the fervent prayers of the last eleven days would avail much! So there you have it! You don't have to believe it…it doesn't matter if you do…you're a part of His wonderful plan, and I'm grateful for what Fb has provided for me. BTW, Chuck is watching TV with me tonight…talking, breathing on his own, and hugging his kids! He's alive!

Thankful,
Sara Stophel

Your Turn

Share about a time when you heard the Lord direct your steps in a way that took a leap of faith. Were you able to put one foot in front of the other and obey? Did God work things out in a way you had not anticipated?

_____

_____

_____

_____

_____

_____

_____

_____

_____

_____

_____

_____

_____

A Song of New Hope

Stophel-darity

❧

"A family that shaves together, stays together."
Sara Stophel

Surely there's some psycho-babble term for the condition when a person's brain returns to the last thing it was doing before a traumatic occurrence. For me, it was a Michael Jackson song. Asher and I had been rocking out to *Wanna Be Startin' Somethin'* when Chuck's desperate call to go to the hospital had come through. For the following two weeks, any time my mind was not sorting out the last doctor's comment or trying to remember an important detail for someone, it was rehearsing over and over, "Too high to get oveh, too low to get undeh, I'm stuck in the middle, and the pain is thundeh...." It got to the point that I was *begging* the Lord to replace those lyrics with a worship song or SOMETHING. It just seemed wrong to be singing that song in my head while my husband was in a dire state! I would come up with another option, only to find myself back at..."mama-see-mama-sah-moo-mah-coo-sah...." UGH!

So, now that Chuck had awakened, we began unfolding the details of the previous ten days, trying hard to spare him too much at once. It was apparent that he was much more confused and concerned about having missed ten days of his life than he was that he almost LOST his life; "Wigged out" was his term for it! Then, Stophel-darity became the theme as my boys and some of Chuck's good friends shaved their heads along with

Chuck right there in CICU...professional cosmetologist and all! Those doctors and nurses had no idea what to do with us!

Days became weeks. Chuck's dad and I took turns sleeping at the hospital on the room's tongue-depressor sized couch. I was always excited when it was my day...it was like an all-night date. I'd fret about what to wear, or how to fix my hair! Just about the time we'd think Chuck was close to going home, something would happen. Back to the CICU. Twice an evasive internal bleed was cause for much concern. Twice more, doctors told me I should bring the boys in to see him just in case he did not recover.

Seven room changes, six weeks, three very close calls, and a personal phone call from Chris Tomlin...Chuck's favorite worship leader/songwriter and...we finally got him home.

Chuck had his first opportunity to write to the Chuck's Butt Kickin' Friends Facebook group a couple of days after getting home. "I cannot even begin to write without tears of amazement and awe at the outpouring of love that has been experienced by my family and me. Thank you seems so inadequate, but every fiber of my being is so overwhelmed...we serve an ASK-tronomical God!" Healing had come, and based on the shocked looks on the faces of several doctors, we knew medicine could not take full credit for the Miracle who came home.

We do serve an ASK-tronomical God...AND, I was finally able to get back on the Michael Jackson horse..."You're a vegetable...you're a vegetable...they haaaayyy-te you...you're a vegetable!!" [6]

---

[6] Jackson, Michael. "Wanna Be Startin' Somethin'," Thriller, 1982.

ChuckFEST

❧

"There is nothing more beautiful than someone who goes out of their way to make life beautiful for others."[7]

Mandy Hale

During the aforementioned hospital crisis, a new friend named Angela visited me to ask permission to hold a fund-raiser on our behalf. First of all…who would say NO to that?! And secondly, what DO you say to such a generous offer without sounding trite? Unfortunately, I had reached "numb"…my answer was of course, "Yes, thank you," but I walked away wishing I'd have looked and sounded more grateful, more thankful, jumped up and down…*something*.

Chuck had been home just a few days when ChuckFEST took place. We arrived at the venue – our younger boys' school – and were COM-PLETELY overwhelmed at the sights. Tables were covered with beautiful baskets full of goodies, autographed books, crafts and art for auction. There were even ChuckFEST T-shirts for sale! Someone had arranged for a dona-tion of one YEAR'S worth of toilet paper and paper towels!! Not gonna lie…we are STILL using the paper towels as of writing this! LeAnne Taylor (local TV celebrity) was MC'ing the event, and the food and schedule of entertainment were top-notch! I overheard a guest saying, "This must be what it's like in Heaven!" Perhaps the most true statement of the day. In that room were people we'd loved for twenty plus years from Christian

---

[7] Hale, Mandy. *The Single Woman: Life, Love, and a Dash of Sass,* Nashville, TN, 2013.

Chapel, people we'd come to know and love from Asbury UMC, families we were just beginning to know from Abiding Harvest UMC, teachers and students from Augustine Christian Academy, and even a handful of nurses from CICU! The event raised over $15,000 that day alone, and monies continued to come in for weeks following. Amazing.

One lady from Chuck's childhood sent a check for $2,000 with a note that said she was not good at praying, but she was good at giving! She asked that we use the money for something other than a medical bill if possible…"Have some fun or get something you WANT instead of NEED." We did just that… I'm happy to say I typed much of this story on that little iPad in its pink case! There was still enough money to take a short trip to Branson with the boys. On the way there I read aloud from the pages and pages of posts on the Chuck's Butt Kickin' Friends Facebook wall. Tears covered Chuck's face with each post, prayer, and encouraging word. My voice would get shaky, but tears wouldn't come. I realized then…it was time to debrief. I was in desperate need of a meltdown. Healing comes through tears, and I had shed very few as of yet.

We were blessed by the McIntyre family, who loaned us a bunch of medical items to help with rehabilitation at home. Chuck had a seat for the shower, a walker, a wheelchair complete with flashing lighted wheels, and for the master bathroom, a raised toilet seat to make our commode about six inches higher. Chuck and I laughed a lot those first days and weeks home from the hospital. The first days we spent alone, after the boys returned to their regular school routines, were full of adventure.

Chuck was so tall and so weak, and I am so short and…so weak! One day he'd made it to the bathroom successfully with his walker, got situated on that raised seat…but found himself unable to get up once finished…

you know, finished...reading! After several attempts to help him stand up, we decided he might be there for the next three hours until one of the older boys could help! That particular piece of rehabilitation equipment provided comedic relief again a few weeks later. Being vertically challenged, I had to reach up on my toes in order to be able to sit on the potty seat. I had become accustomed to doing just that, feet dangling as I...read!

One night Chuck decided he was able to get up and down without that extended seat, and removed it after I'd settled down for the night. Later, I "brailled" my way in the dark to the bathroom. I pulled up my nighty, down my undies, reached up on my tippy-toes, and SLAM! Down I went with a teeth-chattering bang! No more six-inch extended seat! "Guess he's reached a new milestone!"

When Life Gives You Lemons...

"If you say you can or you can't, you're right either way."
Henry Ford

"Peace be with You," Sunday's sermon title, from the scriptures in which Jesus appeared to His followers alive and well after being crucified days before. Perfect message for me at that time. I had the feeling that just around the corner were days where peace would be fleeting. Maybe it's bad to set myself up for that, but I'm what I'd call a *Realist*. I was at the place at which my heart's faith and my head's knowledge had collided. My heart knew God was in control and that He had a plan; however, my head had files and files of memories from the last sixteen years...not to mention from the recent three months! Times are not easy just because God is in control, and if I'm to be honest...it often felt as though He was either NOT in control or just plain mean.

Perhaps I'd reached that point to debrief. Debriefing to me meant... cry, and that had only happened three times in all of the painful moments over the previous months. "For God's sake, Sara! The doctor just told you to bring in your children to say good-bye to their dad...the love of your life...forever! And you just swallowed hard and nodded."

I wasn't sure if a good cry was what I needed, but I was sure of one thing. The other shoe was bound to drop. Shoes come in pairs, and it seemed that historically, if one shoe dropped...the other would follow. We had the shoes of financial provision...college tuition/job. We had a pair of shoes full of the spreading cancer. There was the transplanted heart pair of shoes, but those seemed to be intact!

I knew the old adage…"Worry is payment in advance for something you may never own." Well…maybe so…but sometimes it seemed as though it might be smart to start a savings of sort!

Somewhere in the midst of all of the craziness I had joy…not meaning I was happy every moment…but joy – that deeper, peaceful feeling – was always there. Chuck and I sang all the time during those rough days…"You Are My Sunshine," "My Jesus I Love Thee," the Brady Bunch theme…you name it! In the midst of the storm, in the midst of wavering peace, in the midst of chaos, was inner joy. I think you have to know Jesus to know that very contradictory scenario.

So, after several months of recuperating, Chuck was finally able to undergo chemo again…this time using prophylactic antibiotics to prevent infection. It worked! Hooray!! One September morning, he woke up to find his hair beginning to fall out again. He called Cindy, our favorite photographer, who cleared her schedule for THAT NIGHT so we could do a family session WITH hair! Then…we headed over to my mother's house for a video session with our videographer extraordinaire, Kenneth (KVJ Productions…look him up!!). For those who never knew my Chuck… here's a look at the fantastic man he was. Life was always worth a laugh and a smile. Man, I miss that guy!!

(YouTube: search "Chuck Stophel Lemonade" to get a glimpse of his hair-losing video! http://youtu.be/3nvaxfGFeqg)

Mother's Day

❧

*"Rainbows introduce us to reflections of different,
beautiful possibilities so we never forget
that pain and grief are not the final options in life."*

Aberjhani

Twelve months into this lymphoma diagnosis, we seemed to be just about exactly where we were when it all started. We had learned to treat Chuck with antibiotics to keep infection from becoming rampant without warning; however, in order to allow his body recovery time between chemo treatments, the cancer was never quite under control. We finished the six chemo treatments that were usually enough to combat this type of cancer. We'd even made a trip to MD Anderson in Houston and tried another route they suggested might work. However, by May of 2012, cancer was spreading and Chuck's body was weary. The latest PET Scan was far from "unremarkable," and we had decisions to make...fast. We decided to try another chemo, though it was very aggressive and would likely be rough on his body. That proved true.

The three-day intensive ICE program began with a chemo that can be neurotoxic. Chuck, being the overachiever, took that to new levels. Following day two's dose, Chuck was very confused. He completely stopped talking and would stare as though he had woken up in a foreign country with no idea how he got there. They call it chemo brain; it's common...but this was different. Even the doctor on call became concerned, ordering an

109

MRI of his brain. I spent those nights in the chair next to Chuck's bed, and reminded Jesus that when He missed *His* best friend Lazarus, He raised him from the dead. All I was asking was that Jesus would heal cancer and clear *MY* best friend's mind so he'd return to himself.

Day three, Chuck was moved to CICU as he was literally forgetting to breathe. It was Saturday before Mother's Day, and we were called in once again to "say good-bye" just in case. By this time Chuck had no idea who we were. A speech pathologist came in to do an evaluation, asking all sorts of Yes/No questions. "Is this your wife?"

Chuck shook his head, "No."

"Yes she is! You love her! You've been together a loooong time!"

Again, "No." Can't really express that pain. He looked scared and alone, and I could not even assure him he was safe and loved because he looked at me like a stranger. Before long, he was again put on the ventilator.

Precious Asher came to see Daddy Sunday morning, and brought with him a little Mother's Day surprise for me…and boy, was it a surprise! As flowers are not allowed in the ICU, Asher chose a silk arrangement from Walmart. Memorial Day was just around the corner so flowers were easy to find. Mine was a pretty pink rose bouquet arranged nicely in a plastic vase with a GROUND STAKE at the bottom! There was NO way I could let Chuck awaken from this induced coma to find we had grave flowers in his room! We figured out a way to disguise it!

Facebook was another blessing that day. One of Chuck's colleagues sent me a message reminding me that though Chuck could not express it that day, he would have said how proud he was to share in parenting our boys with me. And even though I'd been unable to be present as much as usual with my boys, *they* understood I was where I needed to be at that time.

What an absolutely lovely thing to do for someone. I will never forget that Facebook note.

Take advantage of the opportunity to bless someone with words when the opportunity presents itself. If something nice comes to mind about someone you pass by...assume it's not your own idea but from God and *say* it! You just can't imagine the joy it might bring, the pain it might relieve, the healing it might be to a heavy heart. Hummm...healing comes as simply as words.

The Power of the Mind

❧

*"Faith consists in believing when it is beyond
the power of reason to believe."*

Voltaire

FACEBOOK ENTRY APRIL 10, 2012:

*"Marilynda would be playing the piano. Alan would do his mime.
Maybe Kenneth would put together a montage of pieces from Chuck's
many TV interviews. Somehow I would have to get "We Will Rock
You" in. If I had it in me, I would say SOMETHING."*

You'd have thought I spent hours thinking about it…Chuck's memorial service, I mean. Truth was, all of those "plans" came to mind in split seconds over this, the next set of scary days. I remember wishing the planning would stop. Was that God? Was He preparing me for what was to come? I'm still not sure about that. One thing I did know…the Chuck in that hospital bed was not the Chuck I'd known and loved for so long. My Chuck made jokes. My Chuck would not ignore me when he saw me cry (or naked!). My Chuck didn't stare blankly. My Chuck was always seeing the bright side and ready for the challenge…whatever it was.

I wonder, how many of *you* are Realists? You know the ones. We are people who love Jesus. We are the people who pray, worship, smile, feel His presence, hear His still, small voice (sometimes), believe in Him, know

Him personally, adore Him with all our hearts, have mustard-seed-sized faith…or even bigger. We are the ones who ask, hope, expect, stand, and sometimes get disappointed. We are the ones who did all we could do and witnessed the death of our sister anyway. We are the ones whose trusters break, and yet we know there is NOTHING better than our Lord, even though we feel He let us down.

You may have heard someone pray and say, "Amen! It's done…so-and-so is healed!" I heard it and honestly, I WANTED to agree and believe it too. The thing is, I HAD that kind of faith when Chuck's heart was so sick. Really, I even told Dr. Ensley I expected God to heal Chuck's heart without surgery. (He didn't even pretend like I was sane for saying that!) Then, God had the nerve to trump me with sovereignty. In spite of my faith, He has the right to execute His will. In spite of a prophetic word spoken over me years before, God did not choose to heal in the way I'd expected. Now that's not to say He doesn't sometimes give us the answer we beg for only to find submission to His direction would have paid off better in the end! We have to make sure our "asking" is not for selfish motives. We have to read His Word as if it were a map and guiding Light. We need to look at precedence in Scripture…the way He works. That's scriptural, and THAT'S for another book! Are you like me? Have you hoped, prayed, and believed and then felt God let you down? Read on….

Nicole to My Rescue

❧

"Sisters function as safety nets in a chaotic world
simply by being there for each other."

Saline

Chuck's little sister, Nicole, flew out to help; and I could not have been happier about it! For one thing, she was able to communicate with Chuck when the rest of us had been unable. She got right down in his face and said with a loud voice, "Chuck, it's your BEAUTIFUL sister Nicole!" He actually looked at her, and a tear ran down his cheek. As much as I wished he'd have known me, it was pure delight to know he recognized someone and would not feel all alone.

She took turns staying nights with the boys or at the hospital so I could rest at home. During her visit, Chuck was again awakened and had the opportunity to spend time with Nicole reminiscing. Well, he wasn't speaking yet, but communication still happened. If she walked out of view, he would search the room and a look of peace came over his eyes when he'd see her again.

Sometime during that week, he began recognizing the boys and me again as well. Whew!

Hours before her flight home, Chuck choked on secretions and began turning blue. Nicole ran for help and all hell broke loose. We sat on the little tongue-depressor sofa and watched as staff rushed around the

115

room, placed the defibrillator pads on Chuck's chest, and began a BiPAP machine. Though his stats dropped low, he was able to recover without being shocked. And so it went…two steps forward and three back. At least that's how it felt.

Our three-day chemo treatment stay had again become weeks, but little by little, Chuck showed improvement. Dr. Ensley and Oncologist, Dr. Strnad…or rather, "Dr. May-I-Buy-A-Vowel" still in the mix, kept Chuck alive so many times when it seemed very unlikely he would make it. Weak and atrophied, Chuck had to learn to walk again. Discussions began about whether or not to move him out of the hospital to some sort of Rehab Center. The very thought of that made me very uncomfortable having had so many setbacks and without warning. The prerequisite was to be off all IV drugs so that therapy could be done without poles in tow.

Chuck's parents were here for a couple of weeks, which made decision making so much easier. The pressure of making so many grown-up decisions alone had taken a toll. At some point it was mentioned that perhaps my complaining about being cold all the time, was in fact, shaking from nerves. After all, it was June! A visit to Dr. Reinking, or Dr. Lionking as we call him, set in motion antianxiety medicine, and you'd be surprised how I seemed to warm up!

My June 1 Facebook post read:

It's been a very weepy day for Chuck. I remember last year, all of the processing after having missed weeks of life, but this is different. Today Chuck grieved over the loss of his best childhood friend, the Best Man in our wedding. He was certain Jeff had died in an accident. I assured him it must have been a dream, even showed him a recent card we'd received from Jeff and his wife. After being told we had missed the wedding of our friend Randy, he asked, "Am I whacked out, or is Randy's husband ALUMINUM??" With every ounce of composure I answered, "Uuhh…you're whacked out!" He would laugh, but then tears would come out of frustration at not knowing reality from dreams. He felt his nights were spent in spiritual warfare. Perhaps they were. We war not against flesh and blood, but against spiritual forces of all kinds. (See Ephesians 6:12.) Please pray for my Chuck to have the mind of Christ.

Over the next days he began to eat, swing his legs over the bed to sit up, and regain enough strength that we were able to have a conjugal visit… NO, not really! But I DID climb up into his bed and watch the Thunder game with him! Chuck's ICU room was a party of shouting and cheering, and I think the night staff was just as thrilled as we were that he was up for that! With that gaining of strength came the realization that he had been unable to make decisions about anything in his own life…and he was going to start now! When a nurse came to draw blood gases, he flat out said, "NO!" She wanted to remove several of the IV lines that were no longer in use. His response, "Forget it!"

For years Chuck and I have said about the Body of Christ…some are hands that heal, some are feet that go, some are knees that intercede…We felt it was often our job to be the butt! Someone has to!! And so I prayed that while questioning and even denying treatment, we would still show the love of God!

An Immeasurable Gift

✦

"No one has ever become poor by giving."

Anne Frank

Sometimes, when I'd sit down to write a Facebook update, I'd think to myself, "This is going to sound so pitiful AGAIN!" But, then there were the days that God did something so unbelievably precious that I couldn't wait to get it on paper…or…on Facebook! This was one such day!

Chuck was once again intubated as chemo had caused terrible sores in his mouth, and the pain made it difficult to cough and keep the lungs clear. We had the promise that he'd be off the vent quickly this time, but the fear and nerves crept in just the same. I left Chuck with a special friend and went home to recharge. While there, I received a text that started a chain of events from which God would show Himself Papa to my sweet Asher.

Over the last year, Asher had researched all about a little creature called a Sugar Glider. He checked out books, watched every YouTube video, and studied comments from exotic pet veterinarians. A text I received from a friend said the local mall had a kiosk with Sugar Gliders and would be there only one more day. We had never seen one in person, and there was no way we were missing this opportunity. On the way to the mall, Asher and I prayed that the Lord would help us to not become too attached or be too disappointed over not bringing one home. Actually, I had decided to scrape up the money and get one for him...even if it cost a hundred dollars!

We arrived in time to watch a little show where these darling creatures would fly (glide) ten feet from a raised hand into the owner's pocket! Precious! Then came the sticker shock. SIX HUNDRED DOLLARS! There went my plan for a surprise. Asher was tough, knowing we could not spend that kind of money on a pet. Pretty sure he handled it better than I. Time came to head back to the hospital, and we walked away feeling downcast while remembering to be thankful we got to see the sweet little guys.

As we walked away my phone rang. It was a number I did not recognize, and I assumed the hospital was calling. Instead, it was Christy, a teenage girl from Augustine Christian Academy. She and her friend had seen us at the kiosk and wanted to let us know they were going to buy a Sugar Glider for Asher!! I burst into tears (which really freaks a kid out when his dad is very ill!)...right there in the mall, sobbing! "No way, that's way too expensive! You can't do that!" But, she had already spoken to her mother and the deal was made.

Those girls could not have known how the night before Asher told me he wondered if God hated him because He was not answering his prayers for his daddy. Another opportunity for me to put into practice the growth I'd seen since Chuck's heart days. So I told Asher that his daddy had honestly said, "I would go through all of this again if someone would come to know Jesus because of it." Now I got to point out that not only did God have to arrange the text telling me the Gliders were in town, but He also had to prompt two teenage girls to go to the mall (okay, that part was easy for Him!), and then speak to their hearts to serve Him by serving a little boy who needed to experience His love.

God is not always practical in His love. Sometimes He just wants to spoil us. A want, not a need. What an extravagant example God displayed to prove my point…thanks, God!

Acayla recently celebrated three years with Asher...cake and all!

No Rest for the Weary

❧

"But those who hope in the Lord will renew their strength. They will soar on wings like eagles: they will run and not grow weary, they will walk and not be faint."

Isaiah 40:31

Room 4203, Therapy Floor, was no piece of cake. Our excitement for Chuck's progress was mixed with pain for his, well…pain. From day one, Chuck was awakened by 6:30 for Occupational Therapy to dress him to his shoes. He had breakfast in the dining room, and then straight to the gym for Physical Therapy. There was no easing into the routine. One day he'd been applauded for sitting up thirty minutes in a chair and the next, expected to hang in there for six hours of various therapies. By evening, when "nature called," I had to literally *hold his head up* so he could use the restroom. It was the first time he'd rated his pain as a ten. The words of Dr. Ensley hung over my head, "How long will you make him suffer?" I don't think he meant ME specifically, maybe he did. I had made it clear to Chuck weeks before that if he reached a point of having had enough, he could go home to Jesus.

The next days showed improvement as Chuck walked with a walker, showered by himself, and began transferring to a wheelchair on his own. The days were rough, but he loved eating in the dining hall and always seemed to be seated with little old ladies! Each of the boys and I took turns sharing a meal with him there.

The time came to address the cancer again, which was still growing as treatment had been postponed once again to allow Chuck to regain strength. On June 20 I wrote:

"Great is Thy faithfulness, Lord, unto me…and Chuck.

Dr. May-I-Buy-A-Vowel Strnad arrived today with news that the cancer around Chuck's collar bone had grown so quickly it actually fractured the bone. No wonder walking with a walker was so incredibly painful. Precious Chuck forged through no matter what. Radiation will be the immediate plan. The goal is to shrink the cancer while waiting approval for a new drug used only for lung cancer. It has proven very successful with the ALK molecule present in Chuck's cancer. Dr Miale, from Chuck's childhood cancer days, has kept up with me via Facebook and reluctantly (due to medical ethics) has answered general questions for wisdom."

Once again, Chuck began refusing food as his throat felt blocked, though the scans showed nothing in that area. We were approved for staying on the therapy floor while undergoing radiation. It couldn't start soon enough.

Back Where We Started

❧

"Be still my soul, the Lord is on thy side.
Bear patiently the cross of grief or pain...."
Katharina von Schlegel

MY JOURNAL ENTRY FROM JUNE 21, 2012:

In my humble opinion, there are times when it's my job, as the butt in
the Body of Christ, to help someone find a little perspective. Over these
last several weeks, I have ridden the elevator with a number of folks
who felt the need to share their troubles with me between floors 1 and
5. I listen, and say, "Bless your hearts"...and have even offered up a
prayer for a couple of them. BUT, last night, when a guy let out a huge
"SSSSSSSIIIIIGGGGGHHH," exclaiming he had been sleeping here
since the weekend...it just flew out of my mouth, "I've been here every
day for SEVEN WEEKS!" (ding, ding – I exit elevator). "Have a nice
evening." Oh, Sara!

Keeping perspective myself, I knew there were many someones, somewhere, who had it much worse than I. That morning we received
great news from Chuck's therapy team that he had been taken to radiology
for the pre-radiation scan...eighteen hours ahead of schedule! We were
thrilled they had jumped on it in spite of its being a Friday.

With a little extra time before our visit, Asher and I had lunch out and ran a couple of errands all while blasting a hymns CD. "Be Still My Soul, the Lord is on thy side…." When we walked into his room, we found him surrounded by medical staff, bed tilted nearly upside down, oxygen flowing, fluids running, and a blood pressure of 72/29. "What the heck happened? Everything was perfect an hour ago!"

Very shortly, we were moved back to CICU. So discouraged and completely frustrated, when Pastor Buskirk walked in I looked him straight in the eye and said, "Ssshh****tttt!" I suppose if you're going to throw out a curse word, saying it to your pastor provides the opportunity for an immediate confession! He'd heard it before, and assured me that the Apostle Paul even referred to those things that we hold significant as, actually, the world's dung! As for Jesus, He'd already heard it in my head and heart, and I'm pretty sure He was giving me one of those "I've gotcha" looks. We have that kind of relationship after all we've been through together over the years.

I was certainly feeling deflated, as was Chuck. Another promise of progress was again crashed into by another moment of setbacks…and nobody could guess for how long. The practice of medicine was about to reach its limit, leaving room for only God to step in with a miracle.

"Be Still My Soul, Thy God doth undertake, to guide the future as He has the past. Thy hope, thy confidence let nothing shake; all now mysterious shall be bright at last. Be still, my soul; the waves and winds still know, His voice Who ruled them while He dwelt below." [8]

---

[8] Von Schlegel, Katharina. "Be Still My Soul", Public Domain. 1752.

$\mathcal{THE}$ Talk

❧

"Giving up is conceding that things will never get better, and that is just not true. Ups and downs are a constant in life, and I've been belted into that roller coaster a thousand times."

Aimee Mullins, Paralympic Athlete

The last few days that my Chuck lived on this earth fit perfectly into the up and down pattern of previous weeks. Radiation may or may not have been presenting similarly to the chemo as Chuck asked some crazy questions, keeping Nikolai and me on our toes. We had to kill two bugs that were crawling around the end of his bed, which is hard to do when only Chuck could SEE the bugs! There were moments where I had to pull out the redhead in me to keep Chuck in CICU. He was much too frail and was unable to find the call button. He had become afraid of choking and afraid to be alone…and those things made me afraid. Things seemed to change by the hour.

June 27th we were given "The Talk"…the one that lets you know there is nothing left that medicine can do. Chuck was determined to continue fighting, and I was determined to fight with him. To our total surprise and delight, Jeff…the Best Man who did NOT die in an accident…walked into Chuck's room! He'd flown in from North Carolina, pictures in hand. They spent the day remembering childhood sleepovers and games of HORSE on the home basketball court. In order to make a one-night sleepover into a two-night sleepover…they'd spell out LYMPHATIC HISTIOCYTOSIS!!

Now THAT'S a basketball game! Jeff did most of the talking, but Chuck was all smiles all day.

———❦———

Back in Florida, Chuck's mother was undergoing heart surgery that she had delayed the month before in order to visit here. We knew God's timing is perfect, but it surely seemed off today. Creston and Nikolai spent the night with Chuck, and I went home with Asher. At about 11:30 p.m., I received a call from the boys that Chuck wanted to have "one of those five-minute conversations." I had no idea what that meant. My mind scrambled as I tried to figure out what I should do, having taken Ambien and knowing Asher would be left home alone if I made the trip to the hospital. Eventually, we figured out Chuck was having another moment of confusion that Jeff and the boys were able to help settle. It was something about his catheter and a Jewish meeting...and in all fairness, that would get ME all in an uproar were I him! (You know how the Hebrews handled that area...just sayin'!)

I settled down to make another attempt at sleep only to receive another call at midnight. It was the head nurse informing me that she would need to follow the patient's last words, wanting to be intubated if that would save his life, but that there was a dispute between doctors. Several of the specialists had been in the room that morning before when Chuck had said he was still in the fight. They had documented his will to continue; however, the doctor who would perform the ventilation procedure was against it, saying the other doctors were presenting "false hope." She wanted me to know, if this took place, I would have to get power of attorney, etc., etc.... and wished me a good night's sleep. Right.

I got up early to be sure I'd be there for morning rounds. Dr. MIBAV Strnad gave his usual "it ain't over 'til it's over" speech, but was honest to say things were not looking good with the morning labs and continued organ failure. By 10:00 the kidney doctor and Hospitalist had explained that Chuck would need to start dialysis ASAP, but would need to be vented again first. They were also concerned he would not survive the procedure to implant a dialysis shunt…and it was important we understand that he could not undergo radiation while on the ventilator. If we fixed one thing, we'd have to ignore another. They left the room asking us to consider our options and let them know.

I asked Jeff to stay and help me understand Chuck, as he was full time on the BiPAP mask by then. Between the two of us, we saw Chuck place his hand on his chest and point to me. "I love you too," I said…though I wasn't sure that's what he meant. He pointed up to God and waved his hands side to side. I asked him, "Are you saying it's up to God?" He nodded yes. I removed the mask long enough to hear him say, "I'm done," and again point up.

Tearfully, I walked out to report the decision. I was told Chuck would receive morphine in small doses, increasing as difficulty breathing increased. "It will take about twenty-four hours." Just like that everything had changed, now he had a 24-hour life prognosis. All three boys returned to the hospital, and Jeff postponed his flight home to be with us. Although he really did not stay in the room much that day, it was nice knowing he was there. Creston and Nikolai preferred we spend the last hours with their dad alone, so I arranged for our Besties to come at 5:00 p.m. to say their good-byes, and sing songs of worship. By noon, however, it was clear that Chuck would not be suffering on this earth much longer, so friends began to gather much sooner. The boys and I held his hands, sang songs… *You are my Sunshine*…and exchanged "I love you's." At one point Chuck motioned to remove his mask and said in a whisper, "I want to sing." Tears running down my cheeks, I told him, "You will be singing soon."

Top, L to R: Creston, Nikolai
Bottom L to R: Asher, Sara and Chuck

Your Turn

Proverbs 17:22 tells us laughter truly IS like a medicine. Are you able to find joy in spite of your circumstances? (Not just happiness...but internal JOY!) Write down a time during a rough-life-patch, when you were able to really laugh, find peace, and feel joy.

_____

_____

_____

_____

_____

_____

_____

A Song of Grief

The Chuck Effect

*"If you would not be forgotten as soon as you are dead, either write
something worth reading or do things worth writing."*

Benjamin Franklin

These are just a few of the precious notes from the Butt Kickers:

"I am deeply grieved, but it is only bye for now." Jamie

"I have not stopped thinking and praying. My heart grieves with you.
What an outstanding life Chuck lived. God must be bursting with pride
over that one!" Abi

"Dear Stophel Family, There isn't a person that Chuck met whose life
he didn't impact in a very good way. You are in my thoughts and prayers."
Sharon

On and on, wonderful notes of encouragement came from the Butt
Kickers day and night. A close family friend started a new page called the
Chuck Effect in which people told stories about how Chuck had impacted
their lives...everything from his singing at a funeral, to the time he led a
man to Jesus days before the man died, to how he stopped on the highway
to help with a flat tire! Each story was a little piece of healing to our broken
hearts. Oh, to hear that so many others recognized the preciousness of our
daddy and husband. Priceless.

With Chuck's Butt Kicking Friends fully engaged and in motion, my journaling became less and less of a private expression in a notebook, to a public expression of all that I thought and felt and experienced in the days following Chuck's move to Heaven. Writing on Facebook became self-therapy, and continued to be a way to keep the Butt Kickers informed about our family. What really surprised me was that my "ability" to share transparently was becoming a source of healing in the hearts of people all over the country, most of whom I've never met. Responses came from people who were relieved to know they were not the only ones with broken trusters. Healing ministry, perhaps, did not mean physical, supernatural healing of bodies...but spiritual and emotional healing of broken hearts and trusters.

"Lord Jesus, let me say and be that which You have called me to say and be, not misleading Your sheep due to my own lacking or faltering faith." That has been my prayer. Many of the following chapters are from those posts that were met with such precious reception by those who have questioned God in the same ways I have. To God be the glory....

A Pincher and a Squeezer

❧

"Kiss me and kiss me again, for your love is sweeter than wine."

Song of Solomon 1:2 NLT

"Were the whole realm of nature mine, that were an offering far too small"…from beneath the covers the harmony would come…"Love so amazing, so divine, demands my soul, my life, my all." I woke up singing hymns often those last six months with my Chuck. And when he had a voice with which to sing, he always joined in. He was so alive right up until the moment he was…well, so much MORE alive!

My mother used to say of my dad, "He's not a pincher or a squeezer." THAT did not apply to my Chuck! Let's just say that forging a staircase ahead of him was dangerous. Flirting was part of our relationship, though certainly more so on his part! It kept things alive and fun, all while making our kids roll their eyes and say, "Gross!" The last time I got to do a little flirting was while he was on the therapy floor. Chuck had made a list of things he wanted brought up to his new room: comfy pants, hand weights (as if he was not getting enough exercise from six hours of daily therapy!), boiled peanuts for a snack, etc. Along with the bag of items requested, I tossed in a black thong! Now, before you start the TMI comments, I never WORE the thing…well, not for any length of time! It was an inside joke and is now between us and several thousand of you! It made him laugh and gave him the umph to push hard that day, shooting for home.

I share all of that so you'll better understand one of our last exchanges before his trip to Heaven. During that last week in ICU, Chuck held on to a suction tube, much like the ones your dentist uses. He was concerned he might choke, and would use it often to clear anything from his mouth to prevent it from going down the wrong way.

While the boys and I were sitting with Chuck those last moments of his earthly life, his "sucker" as we'd begun calling it, suctioned right onto my… chest! He was so weak, I assumed it was accidental. Maybe his arm fell to the side and he couldn't get it back up on the bed. I looked at him to see if he needed help moving it. BUT, alas, he smiled and winked! That man was flirting on his way up to Heaven! His absence sure makes going up the stairs boring! Once in a while I'd wonder if it was appropriate dipping me to kiss in front of the kids or pinching my rear on the stairs, but I realize now that security was promoted in our boys as they witnessed that we had fun together and we loved each other.

I would encourage you, be a pincher and a squeezer for your kids and for your marriage! It might promote another form of healing…healing of a person's self-regard. "I'm worth his/her attention!" You won't regret it!

My Condolences

❧

"Go ahead, make my day!"
Clint Eastwood, Sudden Impact 1983

For the next of kin, those first days following a death are full of decision making, paper signing, and all sorts of questions that I was in no shape to answer. My mother and sister Sue accompanied me to the funeral home to make arrangements; just as we predicted, the funeral director walked in and offered her condolences to MY MOTHER!

After Chuck had been in Heaven for a few days, and when the house was empty, I took a moment to stand in his closet in hopes of smelling something CHUCK. His clothes were snuggled up against my face, but there was nothing. Our darn space age, multilevel marketing, oxidizing-the-water-so-no-scents-survive-the-washing-machine gadget really worked! I finally cried, but I stopped. It was risky to me because there was no guarantee that once started, the tears would ever cease.

Sorting through Chuck's things came little by little. One morning I discovered his hand gun under our bed. It made me pretty uncomfortable, not knowing the status of its barrel. I called a friend from church who was a retired police officer for a little refresher course in gun handling. After hearing my response to his question, "What kind of gun is it?"...I'm pretty sure he came lights and sirens!! *Now* I know it is a semi-automatic, 40 caliber Taurus. In all fairness, I was partially right...it *IS* in fact BLACK!

He suggested we do some practice shooting, and I must say, those innocent silhouettes took a real beating.

SO, for any would-be stalker, burglar types out there...just know, I WILL shoot you in your lame head, being careful to preserve the integrity of any vital organs for donation. THEN, I will check to see if you have prayed to ask Jesus into your heart. What?!?

Help Wanted: Vineyard Keeper

$\sim\!\!\infty\!\!\sim$

*"This is to my Father's glory, that you bear much fruit,
showing yourselves to be my disciples."*

John 15:8

Song of Solomon tells us it's the little foxes that ruin the vineyards. Throughout all of the events Chuck and I shared as husband and wife, there were numerous events that could be considered miraculous, wonderful works of God. Chuck chose to focus on those; I TRIED to focus on those. Truth be told, the "little foxes" got to me more often than not.

During the time he awaited a new heart, Chuck would have blood drawn several times daily. Every day nurses would have to stick him over and over…and over. Why couldn't God provide a nurse who could draw blood from my Chuck? A little fox. Temporary kidney failure robbed us of peace. Even Chuck found that underground dialysis center depressing. Little fox. Constant migraines have plagued me throughout the years. Why? Little fox. Why did Chuck request shampoo when he was bald? (Just checking to see if you're still with me!) Truly though, did all of those little things that caused so much anguish really *do* anything for the Kingdom of God?

And while I'm asking…whose idea was it that, just DAYS following my husband's death, we would be audited for our ministry mileage from both our 2010 and 2011 taxes? Seriously? Were the few miles we drove to sing really causing financial hardship in America?! My brain was at capacity, and now I had ten days to collect receipts, the mileage log, and all calendars showing ministry opportunities across the country, and meet with an agent to prove it all true. How could the Lord allow this now? Has He *no* compassion? Another fox.

That's how I'd been feeling for several days, er…off and on for several months…okay, that's a pattern of feelings I've dealt with for the last twenty years. It seemed as though my truster had finally been repaired, but as it turned out, I am still a cracked pot. It's always easy to trust God on the sunny days.

Sunday, following the arrival of the IRS letters, I dragged myself to church; a rare occasion, as I was not attending much since my widowhood began. The sermon was titled, "Choosing (which he translated as TRUST-ING) Christ with My Frustration." Appropriate, though I admit my first thoughts were that Pastor Davis had probably never lived a frustrating day in his life! He was living out his calling with a beautiful wife and four beautiful daughters who attend his church with their families. He wasn't one to share personal stories much, so as far as I could tell, life was perfect for them.

After those first seven years following Chuck's heart transplant, I had learned to trust the Lord again, little by little. God had won over my heart again, and my truster was pretty well repaired. When hard things happened, I faced them without blaming Him for every one of them…not that I ever thought He CAUSED the bad things…but He did allow them. Even upon this very huge life loss, I had held on to His hands and felt His grace; I was able to trust that somehow God would use this for His glory and not let one single moment of Chuck's pain be for naught. It seems like the big things are easier to hand over to the Lord. It's the little things that I often felt like He allowed my way, those little foxes nibbling at the vine that invariably stole my joy. Does God have redemption planned for the vines eaten by little foxes?

ALL things work for the good of those called according to His purpose (Romans 8:28). Is this sermon saying I am supposed to believe that FALLING APART while being audited in the middle of grieving my husband is just a "frustration" to hand over to God? Is he saying that STRESSING over the to-do list for Nikolai's graduation actually just needs to be placed at the foot of the cross? So I shouldn't be SWEATING the fact that I may need to find another job, or STRIVING to make sure my diabetic son takes his insulin on time? Those things are all just a "journey away from peace, joy, and rest"? That is, in fact, what he was saying. Well, what did HE know?! And how exactly is that done? I needed to keep the super glue close by as this truster was at risk of shattering…again. I listened intently that morning, and just as I was feeling a renewed sense of strength and faith, Pastor Davis ended his sermon by asking the *perspective questions* of all questions from Hebrews 12:4: "Have you struggled to the point of sweating blood? Have you been sawed in half?"

Crap! "No…but neither have YOU!!"

And so, I did me some talkin' to the Son, and He gave me the Job speech, "Where were YOU when I laid the earth's foundation? Since you know so much, tell Me, how many clouds are up there right now? Have YOU ever told the lightning where to go?" I asked forgiveness for sinning in my anger, and we restored our friendship…again.

I still find myself thinking that way from time to time…it's the TRUSTER issue. But, I'm much more attentive to the tender voice of the Lord reminding me that it's not just MY story going on here…and it's not just Chuck's story. Each "fox" represented another life involved in our story. I pray that the little foxes which challenged us and helped develop the fruit of the Spirit in *our* lives, (love, joy, peace, patience, kindness, goodness, faithfulness, gentleness, and self-control) were situations those connected from the other side see as growth or fruit in *their* lives as well.

Mark 4:11 from *The Message* became Chuck's favorite passage. "You've been given insight into God's kingdom – you *know* how it works. But to those who can't see it YET, everything comes in stories, creating readiness, nudging them toward receptive insight."

Our story interweaves with the stories of nurses who struggled with their ability to draw a man's blood...including the story of the male nurse whom I made cry after FIVE sticks! "OKAY, you're finished here. Go get another nurse!"

Our story connects to Dr. Ensley's story..."We don't ever want to hear from your mouth again, 'Chuck could easily kick the bucket, keel over, or buy the farm'...that is unprofessional!!" He needed to hear that...and I needed to say it! Perhaps we were part of his growth as a doctor...absolutely we share in his life story and he in ours.

We are permanently woven into the story of Dr. "May-I-Buy-A-Vowel" Strnad's life story, and with the story of the gal at Quik Trip who noticed Chuck had not been in for a diet Coke. She cried when I told her he was drinking diet Coke in Heaven now. Our stories connect with an IRS auditor, and car shop owner, with the Sugar Glider manager, with a headache specialist, and even WAY back to the days of our wedding planning while grieving my sister...our stories were woven into the stories of others. There seemed to be a common thread running all throughout my life and Chuck's, and it tied into a desire to understand God and His ways as a Healer. What we were finding is that healing was so much more broad than we understood at all. Now our story of healing is interwoven into yours... and yours into mine.

"Be bold and courageous with your story, do not be terrified, do not be discouraged...for the Lord your God is with you wherever you go!" (Saraphrase from Joshua 1:9). I hope that you will choose, like my Chuck, to see the little foxes as God's way to weave your story into the story of someone else who is being "nudged toward receptive insight." I, too, am working on that. He nudges me a lot!

That Awkward Moment When...

❧

"The finest clothing made is a person's own skin, but, of course, society demands something more than this."

Mark Twain

"That awkward moment when...," a phrase used often in social media. It comes right before a most embarrassing moment or a story about a situation that has no precedent for guidance. For example, that awkward moment when you arrive at the home of your close friend's widow, a member of your church flock, to look through his closet for items you might "want." There's no precedent for that, no school lesson to prepare you; but, it happened one day between sweet Pastor Chris and me.

The thought of strangers pawing through my Chuck's clothing at a garage sale...offering 50 cents for his treasured artsy shirts or slick sport coat, was more than I could handle. I'd much rather have just given it all away. So, I e-mailed Pastor Chris Buskirk to let him know that my boys and I had noticed he was very close in size to Chuck and perhaps he would care to look through his clothes. Most of Chuck's close friends are vertically challenged, or larger in other ways, but Pastor Chris seemed about right, and had that knack for dressing snazzy too! It took him a few days to contemplate, but then he came.

I had things ready...TV on for noise, lights on, and shades up, etc. We made small talk for a few minutes, and then I left him alone. Honestly,

I don't think he really WANTED anything...but how do you say "no" without sounding like you didn't like your friend's taste in clothing, or you aren't the type to wear the clothes of a dead friend...or any number of other thoughts that might hurt the feelings of his widow? And on MY end... how do you make sure the guy knows it's really OKAY if he doesn't take anything, or if he takes it all!? What exactly IS the right way to show your pastor into your bedroom? Pretty sure there isn't a right way for that...so I kept my distance!

I kept myself busy in the kitchen, and read my YouBible, all the while hearing the clinking of hangers and wondering if he felt as weird as I did. At one point, he hollered out that the shirts seemed to be too small around the neck. OKAY, he has an out. But, he kept looking and I kept fidgeting! A good while later, he came out with a sort of contrite look, hoping he had not chosen too much! WHEW! What a relief! I could not have been more pleased, and I know Chuck would have been as well. He loved Chris very much and would likely have told him he looked ALMOST as good in those shirts as he did himself! One more adventure met and conquered. Strangely enough, THAT too was a piece in the puzzle of healing my heart.

It's a Process

"Intelligence is like underwear...It is important that you have it but not necessary that you show it off."

Unknown

The Process. Evidently, that's what it's called when you're walking through the steps of grief. There are four steps, or five, depending on who's writing about it...but I'll be damned if anyone is going to tell me how to grieve! (Even if it DOES happen that way!) Never in all of the grief booklets does it say, "Step 6: You won't know how to dress yourself."

Maybe it's just me. I was dressing for a parent/teacher conference, followed by a staff luncheon at my place of employment. I threw on a top I'd picked up at Walmart several weeks before...one of those, "this looks kinda cute for being a size larger than usual" shirts. I'd worn it to the hospital a few times. It was sleeveless, and the shoulders were cut in such a way that my bra straps often showed. Weeks before, that made no difference to me. As a matter of fact, I wore a hot pink bra to match the hues in the material. Cute and a little sexy for being from my fat clothes collection! However, that day, after Chuck's change of address, a whole new array of thoughts crossed my mind when I looked in the mirror.

"That is completely inappropriate for a widow and single mother!"

"Your boys will think you're trying to find a new man!"

Crazy? Or…is THAT also part of the process? So, I wore a hot pink sweater all day to cover up that potentially sleazy outfit…never mind that it was 105 degrees in Tulsa that day!

Then, on to the next step in the process…retrieving Chuck's ashes from the funeral home. Over the twenty-three years we were together, the idea of tossing our ashes over the beautiful North Carolina Mountain on which his parents' home sits came into our conversation. Following Chuck's change of address, they agreed to have a special spot near the cabin ready for interment where we could all be there together. Chuck was cremated along with a few special mementoes from the boys and me. Creston put in a ball cap from the days Chuck had coached his team; Asher, a stuffed eagle representing Chuck's Eagle Scout Award; I chose to add the last Valentine's card I'd written him; but Nikolai hit the nail on the head…he put in Chuck's favorite thing ~ Chick Fil-A sauce!

I went alone to pick up the ashes. It proved to be much more difficult than I'd expected. I was escorted to a room full of sample headstones and urns, and the wait was long enough that I had time to read them all. When the director came in, she handed me a velvet bag with a heavy box inside and said, "Heeee-re's your honey!" I felt like I might throw up.

From behind her back, she pulled a single bud vase with a pink rose… "He'd want you to have this." I sat in my car and cried…and at the same time, I laughed at myself for wondering if I should seat belt "my honey" in! Another step in the process complete. I think it's my mission to tell grievers about all of the STEPS that nobody ever mentions…like shopping for underwear, about which you've already heard! Who knew?

'Til Death Do Us Part

✑

"Tomorrow morning if you wake up and the sun does not appear,
I will be here...."

Steven Curtis Chapman

Anger is said to be one of those "steps" on that famous grief ladder. I suppose this letter displayed anger, or at least frustration. Somehow, though I knew he'd never read it, writing it released emotions that needed to soar.

JOURNAL ENTRY, SEPTEMBER 10, 2012:

My Precious Chuck,

This week I have missed you so much more than any days before, and though each one expresses it differently, I'm pretty sure the boys feel the same way. Everything we did is another thing done without you. Walmart is one Chuck product after another. New England Clam Chowder, which for twenty-three years made me gag to prepare, somehow seemed worth tasting just to be sure. Heinz 57 practically asked me to take it home, but no one here eats that anymore. Rest assured, we are still able to keep the Kraft Company in business as Asher has your love for cheese, but those canned boiled peanuts will be

---

[9] Chapman, Steven Curtis. "I Will Be Here." By Steven Curtis Chaptman. More to This Life. Sparrow Records, 1989.

off the shelves soon as I'm certain you are the ONLY person in Tulsa who ever bought them.

This week songs have practically shouted at me. "I'm that duet you and Chuck sang at so-and-so's wedding!!"

"Remember me? I'm the song you and Chuck led in worship together at Asbury."

"Oh, Chuck loved singing me!"

And just to top it off, I woke up one morning, checked Facebook on my phone and found the words to "I Will Be Here" tenderly posted on the wall of a young couple in love. We sang that together. You sang it to me..."Tomorrow morning if we wake up and the future is unclear, I will be here. If in the dark you lose sight of hope, hold my hand and have no fear...I will be here."[10] And for the first time I felt like you were not keeping your part of the deal. You are supposed to be here. I am supposed to have a twenty-fifth anniversary...the only Rinehart girl to have that honor. You are supposed to be the one who gets on the boys for not taking out the trash. It's your job to tell them to mow the grass, or to teach them how to change the oil in their cars. That's not my job!

Do you know how many times over the last two weeks someone has said to me, "Get those boys to help you, Sara!"?

"Tell them to just get online and figure out how to put in an alternator...you can do that...save the money...."

Well, that's your job. You tell them. Our neighbor came by this morning. While doing his garage sale last weekend, he heard that you were gone. He asked me why I didn't tell him; I'm pretty sure the sarcasm came across..."Well, I wasn't sure how many doors to knock on and announce

---

[10] Ibid.

my husband's death...I mean, what's the norm for that? Three doors each direction?" He also had suggestions about the boys and their driving fast in the neighborhood. What I wanted to say...never mind, you can guess.

Sigh, Chuck. "Until death do us part"...nobody really thinks that will happen. A couple of weeks ago, I came across the letters we wrote at a marriage seminar where we were the musical guests. We were told to write a letter expressing the things we would have wished were said, were the other to pass away. Your letter said there was a fog covering the sun that used to shine so brightly in your heart. You were right, only I am the one in the fog. Strangely enough, I signed my letter, "I will be here...." Well, I am...and I will be here for our boys, to the best of my ability and for our Lord, though I feel so useless at the moment. I will be here until the Lord calls me home...or perhaps comes to get us all. I know you would say to me, "I will be here" too. Take care of my mansion! I miss you.

Your Sara

Funny how spilling your heart, whether in anger or happiness, tears or laughter, sarcasm or telling it straight...it all fosters healing.

Interpretation Is a Gift of the Spirit: I Don't Have It

❧

"The color of someone's skin doesn't tell you nearly as much about them as the color of their nail polish."

Sassycards.com

It had been two months since our world changed, and I finally decided to pamper myself a little. I arrived at the local nail salon, and that knot-in-my-stomach feeling that has become so familiar began forming. I'll admit it, I have an issue with Asian people. I mean, they're great! I have Asian friends…it's just that, I don't seem to have the gift of interpretation with that particular accent. The day went like this:

Vietnamese Girl: "Pee collah."

Me: "Excuse me?"

VG: "Pee collah" (pointing to the wall of polishes).

Me: "Oh, okay. (I made my way over to choose from the 50 shades of red.)

VG: "July?"

Me: "No, I've never been here before."

VG: "July?" (pointing to my color choice).

Me: "Well, I'm going to wear it in August."

VG: (frustrated) "JU-LY COLLAH?!"

Me: "Oh, yes! I like the color! (That's why I pee the collah!)

We didn't say much after that; forty-five minutes is a long time to hold the hands of someone with whom you cannot communicate! "How will I ever minister healing to one of *these* people, Lord? My ears don't make the cut!" I wanted so to be available!

August presented other new realizations as I returned to work after four months away. Every day after work, Chuck or I would call the other to catch up on the day so far. My first day back, I sat down in my car, hooked the seat belt, and reached for my phone. Then it hit me…I no longer had someone with whom to share my day. It's that newsy stuff, like what funny thing happened in my classroom, or whose little nose left boogers on my shirt. Who on staff is new, or what is God doing in the life of a good friend. I COULD share that stuff with my boys and they would listen, but they wouldn't care like my Chuck did. Nobody would care like a spouse. I have some wonderful girlfriends…but I wouldn't care to hear about THEIR workday most of the time either!

During those first days back at work, someone mentioned her ten-year goal. TEN…YEARS. I went there: ten years of Valentine's Days, ten years of "Dinners for Eight" at church, or in my case, "Dinner for Seven," ten years of keeping my daily activities to myself. I'm not sure my mind had really grasped the fact that Chuck would not be back. Somewhere down inside I think I expected him to walk in just in time for dinner. As a matter of fact, a couple of times I heard the front door open and thought for a split second, "He's home." Ten years.

Then there's that possibility that "something could happen" with me in that ten years, though it would take one heck of a guy to keep up with this princess! The family refers to that possibility as Boaz, after the biblical man who rescued a widow. It would take a pretty special Boaz for sure. Asher read over my shoulder as I filled out paperwork one day, and when I checked the box for *widow*, he responded from behind, "And keep it that way!" Only God knows what the next ten years hold; that's a good thing, I'm not certain I want to know...but I DO want Him to know I'm here to be used as He has desired...at least I'm *trying* to make myself available to Him!

I continued holding hands with Asian folk every two weeks for about a year, without ever feeling like I got to minister to them. Eventually, wisdom said my nails were a luxury I could no longer afford. When I asked to have them removed, the nail guy tried adamantly to talk me out of it.

Vietnamese Nail Guy: "What you have done today?"

Me: "Well, I need to have my nails removed."

VNG: "You not like pree nails now?"

Me: "Oh, yes, I like them, but I need to be smarter with my money."

VNG: "Why? Yo husban not pay fo you?"

Me: (here it goes) "...My husband died." (All ears now attending to our conversation.)

PAUSE

VNG: "You not got a shu-gah-daddy?"

ME: "Weeellll..." (hoping to lighten the mood)…"not yet!"

An Opportunity to Step Out

❧

"[He] comforts us in all our troubles so that we can comfort those in any trouble with the comfort we ourselves receive from God."

2 Corinthians 1:4

Those first days and months proved draining at best. Once home from work, I'd be physically and emotionally spent. My brain was foggy, to the point that I not only left my keys in the car, but actually left my car RUNNING in the Sam's parking lot while I shopped! I'd be exhausted to the point I hurt physically. Then, for some reason, I'd have a day that I just couldn't stop. Busy, busy, busy. I guess that's a coping thing. So having put it off long enough, the time came to mail Chuck's ashes to North Carolina for the approaching interment on the beautiful piece of land his parent's owned where they lived six months out of the year. It was a place that was special to both Chuck and me and now would be his resting place.

That October held many days of milestones. First, I packed up my "Honey" and headed out to send him by U.S. Mail. The guy had to do his usual questioning as to the contents…"Are the contents fragile? Any chemicals? Flammable? Explosive? Do you want to insure your package?… or have an arrival confirmation?"

My face must have shown a complete lack of decision-making skills! I think I just stared at the guy until he finally asked if he could advise

157

me based on the contents of the package. "It's my husband…I mean, his ashes." I'm pretty sure he wished he hadn't asked!

The following day a woman was scheduled to collect the last of Chuck's wardrobe. She was delivering them to an area in Tulsa County that had suffered huge loss due to fires the previous months. I must say, there are some well-dressed country folk out there now! Chuck was GQ head to toe!

Then…I felt the Lord's call to step out and begin to minister to others with the comfort I had received myself. The first opportunity came in an unexpected way.

So what would you think if your boss, or in my case the Director of Education and the CEO, called you out of your classroom in the middle of a school day? Concern for your job? A notice of bad news? Since it was so unusual it might have made sense to have concern or questions. But with my brain working only on a moment-to-moment basis, nothing even crossed my mind! I just walked out to meet them in the hall. I could see they did not want to make their request, but with tears in their eyes, my bosses asked me if I could minister to a mother of four little ones whose husband was very close to death's door.

I don't know what I said in that little chapel, and later I thought of twenty things I WISHED I'd said. But I was able to offer up a prayer and had an empathetic ear. God provided the grace…until about ten minutes after we were finished at which time I broke out in a cold sweat! It had been both precious and heartbreaking, but what God did for me that morning was remind me that He would make use of the pain Chuck had suffered. He would not let go to waste the loss my boys and I still felt. He had a plan. I just had to walk in it.

That is a word to each of us. *You* just have to walk in it…spreading the comfort you have yourself received.

For Everything There Is a Season

❧

"A time to be born and a time to die...a time to weep and a time to laugh, a time to mourn and a time to dance."

Ecclesiastes 3:2,4

The boys and I packed up and flew to North Carolina for the special service on the mountain. None of us had done this before, so I prayed for the Lord to give us the words...or the silence...whichever was right at the time. Nicole's husband Jerry had fashioned a lovely wooden box for the ashes, and Charles fixed a beautiful spot on the mountain where we could sit on a bench and remember. My prayers, too, were that I would be able to help his family understand how Chuck went from "fighting" to "I'm done" in twenty-four hours.

I had been warned there was a list of questions that needed answers. Barbara had not even wanted to speak to me for the first eleven days after Chuck moved to Heaven. For all I knew, she blamed me. I was, after all, the one juggling the faith and healing thing. Due to her heart surgery, they were unable to travel for a memorial service for quite some time, and though we planned to delay it, they insisted we go ahead. This would be my first opportunity to help them find some semblance of peace.

———

Picture a quaint cabin set on the side of the Blue Ridge Mountain range, its Carolina blue roof hidden only a few more weeks by the multicolored leaves on the trees. About 100 yards of neatly mowed grass met at the top of a hill behind the house where a sweet wooden cross marked the resting place of my Chuck. The boys carried the box, placed it in the ground, and covered it with dirt and mulch. Charles announced this would be the third and final memorial service for Chuck…three was enough!! It was a good break in the tension and helped us get going on whatever it was we were supposed to do next!

Barbara shared first her favorite story displaying the kind of person Chuck was. He was seven years old, facing his first battle with cancer. One morning, as they made the trip from Tallahassee to Gainesville for chemo, she asked Chuck how he felt about having cancer, losing his hair, and having chemo. His response showed the selfless Chuck I knew and loved. "I wish I had a twin, and you had adopted him instead, so you wouldn't have to go through all of this." Seven years old.

Nicole went next, reading a tenderly written letter of love she had composed for him. Most precious to me was her memory of being there for Chuck when he was confused and felt alone. I treasure that she was there too. The boys had spoken at the Tulsa service and took a pass this time, so I went next. Chuck and I had an ongoing game to one-up the other about our deep, mushy love. "You are the gravy on my potatoes, you are the bacon with my egg, you are the bubbles in my bathtub"…well, you get the picture!

Charles finished up by praying a blessing over our family from Numbers 6:24-26. "The Lord bless you and keep you; the Lord make His face shine upon you and be gracious to you; the Lord turn His face toward you and give you peace." We received that blessing.

We took pictures, which seemed weird, but we live far away and knew we'd want to see "The Spot" once in a while. Each of us visited that spot on the mountain over the next couple of days…we cling to the hope that we will see him again. For now, Chuck, you are the soft in my tissue.

He Called Me His

❧

"...I just call you, Mine."[11]

David Phelps

"Therefore, since we are surrounded by such a great cloud of witnesses...." Oh, how I WANT to believe that means Chuck is right here...watching, helping, laughing, and crying with me. I want to believe that I smell him...his cologne. I want to believe that he laughed at me when I dropped those airplane peanuts down my blouse...or that he has prayed for me when my head hurts so much. I want so very much to believe he was talking to me, singing to me on that North Carolina mountain. I had climbed up that grassy hill and sat on the ground next to The Spot. There were no sounds except that of the leaves blowing in the breeze.

"Turn your eyes upon Jesus..." I sang.

"Because He lives, I can face tomorrow...."

"And anytime I don't know wha-at to do, I will cast all my cares upon You."

My own little church service right there on the mountain. One chorus after another, I sang and sang.

"I fall apart, and just a word from you somehow seems to fix whatever's wrong. You reach into the weakest moments and remind me that

---

[11] Phelps, David. "I Just Call You Mine." By Jess Cates, Ty Lacy and Dennis Matkosky. The Voice, 2008.

I'm strong. You've gotta know, I'd be a fool not to see, or even worse…to forget, you're more than I deserve."[12] David Phelps, Chuck's man crush! I hadn't heard that song in a while, but it came to mind…only this time it was different. I got the feeling that Chuck was singing to ME. Yeah, I know, Skeptical Sara…I think everything not fully disclosed is an Amway meeting about to unfold!

"Everyone who sees you always wants to know you, and everyone who knows you always has a smile! You're a standing ovation…after years of waiting for a chance to shine. Everyone calls you amazing, but I just call you, Mine."[13] It's really awkward to even type that as it's leaning toward pretty self-indulgent (as Simon Cowell would say!). Still, I was certain SOMEONE was singing to me on that mountain. Why wasn't it enough to know the God of the universe could have been singing to me? I wanted it to be my Chuck. The Bible verse I quoted above comes from Hebrews and according to my research, does not really translate as "spectators" watching us from Heaven, but more like Examples of the Faith; the heroes who have left testimonies of God's amazing grace to which we now cling are our inspiration to finish our races. Whoever it was singing to me that morning…he (or He) had one more thing to say.

"Sara, it's time to take your boys back to church." Church is hard. It's a place that screams, "Chuck isn't here anymore!!" But, we went and we survived. The first sermon we heard following the loss of our patriarch from cancer was about…healing! Seriously, God?!

I'm not really a standing ovation, and surely not everyone calls me amazing…but I AM going to bed these days knowing SOMEONE called me His.

---

[12] Ibid.
[13] Ibid.

Dr. Lionking

❧

"Hakuna Matata, It means no worries!"

Disney's The Lion King

In a moment of insanity, of which I have had many, I scheduled a physical exam for November. At the time, it was February, and I knew there was plenty of time to cancel; however, the whole thing completely slipped my mind until I heard the dreaded message the night before…"Begin fasting at 10:00 p.m., and arrive early for paperwork." How could November have come already?! Too late to cancel.

I was taken to my room and while left to dress…or rather, undress…I gathered up all the confidence I could gather to tell the nurse I would NOT be having THAT test done this time!! After all, my doctor and I had attended worship together for some time! Plus…I don't do much that I don't want to do…especially as of late! She came in ready to take vitals and ask questions, and somehow I felt more naked in my paper gown than if I had just been…naked. My confidence wilted some, but I made my announcement and she seemed fine with it, only to totally betray me to the doctor moments later!

Dr. Lionking came in ready to pounce! He gave me the, "You've been the caretaker for a long time, now you have to take care of yourself" speech. He'd have been better off to have stopped there, but added that my BMI had reached the obese level but, not to worry…"Most of America is at that level!" He then gave me five "DON'TS" to take off the extra weight using his hand as points. Before the end of the day I had DONE each point...all four fingers and the thumb! He listened to my heart...definitely broken... and looked in my ears, updated my inoculations, and took my blood. He sent me home with an envelope in which I was to return a stool...ours is pretty rickety and I wasn't sure how it would fit, but it would have to do! (Poor guy who opens THAT mail!)

In the end, I was submissive to ALL the tests, and I left very thankful for a doctor who listens and genuinely cares for me and for my boys as he did for my Chuck. He hugged me and even kissed my cheek and I felt well. That's why he is Oklahoma Physician of the Year! I am proud of him! I learned my lesson too. When asked to schedule my yearly physical again...I had to...uhh...check my calendar! Never mind that it's in my phone! Not tricking me into that again!! Healing...through preventive medicine, but in this case and for me...only when needed!

Tears in My Ears

❧

*"When asked if my cup is half-full or half-empty my only response is
that I am thankful I have a cup."*

Sam Lefkowitz

And so November continued, and it was bound to happen…Thanksgiving. There are many things for which I am thankful. I read those daily Thankful Lists on Facebook during the month of November, posted by folks all across the country. The first Thanksgiving without Chuck…I guess I just didn't feel like saying it aloud. I didn't want to play the "let's say what we're thankful for" game at the dinner table. It's not that I'm not thankful. I could list so many things that blessed me personally and blessed our family this year…let alone, the six months we had Chuck that we might not have.

Wednesday, November 21, 2012 Journal Entry:

Today, I woke up pretty blue which doesn't happen often, but it hit hard today. Tears were flowing like Niagara Falls. They just wouldn't stop! At 10:15 I was scheduled to have my broken tooth fixed. Tears still flowing. I walked in trying to get it together, but had to update my profile papers. Insurance: canceled, husband: deceased. They gave me tissues…I continued to cry. Dr. Hughes asked if I was up to it, but I really had no option; my tongue was raw from rubbing the sharp, broken tooth and this was a long holiday weekend. So, on we went…

my seat reclined, tears rolling down my cheeks and into my ears! I finally seemed to pull myself together only to go out to pay the bill and be told, "Dr. Hughes says no charge today…Happy Thanksgiving!" That started the tears all over again!

Giving thanks is biblical, and it's important. I encourage you to do it! But, if you have a day like I did, a day when all that you're thankful for seems small compared to the great loss you feel…I think it's OKAY. God knew my heart, and He knows yours even better than you know your own. Grab a sheet of paper and write down what's on your heart…the good and the bad. List those things for which you are thankful. Read it later when your joy is not being outweighed by your grief. It still counts! Thankfulness results in healing too.

YOUR TURN

Little foxes often did me in! List a few little foxes AND the people whose life stories are now interwoven with yours. Lift up a prayer for them. You've encountered each other as part of a much larger Story!

_____

_____

_____

_____

_____

_____

_____

_____

If you are grieving a loss, whether it be a loved one, a job, or a dream... let God in on it. Express your heart in a written prayer, and if you're able, share it with someone close. Then please, find a support group, join a home fellowship, or at least choose a person in whom you can confide.

_____

_____

_____

_____

_____

_____

_____

_____

A New Song

He Shall Feed His Flock

❦

"Shout out to balloons for basically just being a bag of bad breath."

Unknown

Throughout this whole ordeal, my workplace and co-workers at Little Light House have been a constant in my life. It's the most amazing place on earth, full of the most amazing women (and one volunteer man who works more hours than I!). These people love Jesus and serve Him faithfully with their whole lives.

As a ministry we are always challenged to be in continual spiritual growth, and part of growing in the Lord is taking care of our Temples. This happened as we began our first ever Healthier You Challenge (January 29, 2013 post):

By 5:00 CST today, I have to have set a goal in the Healthier You Challenge in which I am participating at work. In order to receive points and remain on the island, so to speak, I need to announce that goal to our leader and at least one other person. Here's the deal. Setting goals is extremely difficult for me as of late. I try…I think…wonder…ponder, evaluate, and consider options, and then have NO skill in making a decision. It's just not there! It sounds crazy but it's real; deciding between McDonald's and Burger King could send me over the edge! So, I prayed and let my team know I'd have a goal by the end of the "fiscal week"…in two hours! Sunday morning, as I was brushing my teeth, the Lord said,

"Sara…THIS is your goal." Let me just say, my first thought was not, "Wow, Lord…that's so easy!" But more like, "There's NO way in hell I'm telling anyone that I haven't been brushing my teeth at night!" For the record, I'd recently been praised about my lovely gums at the dentist! I have continued to brush in the morning or before going out somewhere, but before bed…I have just climbed up my step ladder onto my princess bed and gone to sleep…halitosis and all!

It didn't matter anyway. Nobody was kissing me goodnight, nobody was there to snuggle, so who would care?! But the Lord showed me that day that HE cared. Not brushing my teeth every night as I always had, was just another step towards not caring about Sara because there's not a Chuck to care about Sara…and THAT was not OKAY with God. Funny how little things like that make deposits in the jar of Love in your heart! I started brushing my teeth again at night, and started waking up more and more wishing to taste and see that the Lord is good!

———

One of the things that makes working at the Little Light House so special is our daily, morning meeting. We call it Flock. It's the twenty-five minutes of prayer, Bible study, and devotional time right before our day serving the Little Ones. Recently, the topic was, "How big is your God?" Our leader for the day held up posters, one with a huge *GOD* in the middle and one with a tiny *god* in the middle and asked us to shout out ways we see our God as big. "Through prayer," "His Word," "Time," "Trust," "Provision," etc. Then, the same directions for reasons our God seems small: "Lack of faith," "Pride," "Self-reliance." I shouted out, "Precedence!"

Precedence. For a number of years, I lived representing both signs. I stood on stages all over the country encouraging people that God was big enough to do ALL the fixing and be ALL the answers for whatever issue they faced. I knew it to be true ~ for them. Based on precedence, He had not acted big for me…at least not in ways I could SEE. Surely He has done much behind the scenes…prevented accidents, or stopped disease, for a while. I had seen miracles with my own eyes…in the lives of others. Most recently, I had been blessed with provision…at the loss of my husband. Don't get me wrong, I'm not in the place now of seeing my God as tiny. We have an understanding, He and I. I gripe about what's happened in my life, and He reminds me who hung the moon! I remind Him how I work for a ministry, and He reminds me how a chemo kid and a kid with a sickly heart grew up to make three boys. Somewhere in there are at least two miracles!

Precedence made it hard for me to trust God. Precedence set me up to struggle with submission to sovereignty. But, it is because of the precedence of loss…the precedence of unrelenting "attacks" (if you will)…and therefore the unrelenting GRACE of God…that I have compassion for "The Lost." The Lost, like, the really angry, hurt by the Church…"Christians suck" kind of lost. I'm talking about compassion for brokenhearted gay kids, understanding of the angry at God kind of folk. Having felt betrayed by God myself, I understand people with hearts broken by Sovereignty's Trump. I get it when people who are "good" wonder why we need a God. The reason my God is so big is because He never gives up on me. When the Bible says His grace is sufficient, it doesn't just mean sufficient to help me make it through my personal hell. I think it also means…His grace keeps going even when He'd like to kick my butt down to hell for a couple of hours to show me how really bad it COULD be! He's so gracious He puts up with me!

My prayer is that God will be huge enough that whatever precedence He has shown…or you have created…whatever sovereignty you've experienced, be it a yes or no to a prayer request, whatever area in your life in which you've felt God *trumped*…you will be still and know He is God. You will learn, like I am, that relationship with Him brings oneness with Him. And that oneness makes our hearts hear and feel His heart. I hope you'll know that He loves you so much that "He stepped down off His throne into the cosmos His own hands had made"[14] so He could relate to you in very personal ways.

---

[14] Phelps, David "One Wintry Night." By David Phelps. One Wintry Night. Word Records, 2007.

Stars Below

❧

"Suck it up, Princess!"

Kidspot

I'd be amiss if I failed to mention the many ways God reached out to me during those first months and now years of Chuck's change of address. There were the meals cooked, the calls and cards sent, and cars worked on by husbands of friends; each gift wonderful and timed graciously by the Lord just as I had need. At some point I stepped out of my comfort zone and asked that Marilyn, a lady from church, help me choose a new bed covering for my room. I had known her for many years, but not in a very personal way, really. Chuck was the outgoing, know everyone and what they drive type!

She responded and before long we were en route to shop for a hot pink and brown combo for my room. Marilyn is a gifted decorator, and I think the wheels were turning long before I caught on! Within a short time, she not only helped choose new bedding, but she had made decorative pillows, a shower curtain, painted walls and cupboards, bought me a ceiling fan/light...and had her husband working round the clock too! With her help and the gift of a gentleman from church, the lyrics to a favorite song were torch-blown onto the wall above my bed.

"We'll dance on stars below. And walk down streets of gold. It'll take at least a million years just to see how far they go. Forever and ever dancing on stars below."[15]

Those words brought such comfort in the dark of night, when the pain of loss was unbearable. One night, just weeks before Chuck's last hospital stay, we had stretched out on the trampoline under the starry sky, and I sang that song to him...every word...and we reminisced about loved ones who were seeing those same stars from above. Now, the chorus was a centerpiece in my newly decorated, princess-like haven.

Once my room was finished...well, the rest of the house seemed so out of date! One by one, we conquered rooms, cleaning and sorting, replacing broken and hand-me-down furniture, painting and updating. Marilyn and Ed spent months with me, and we grew a friendship unlike others I have ever had. She is the tough-love kinda gal...just what I needed; tough enough to help me move forward and gentle enough to know when to hold back! Through Marilyn, I realized the princess in me was still alive and active! It wasn't just the pretend princess who gazed at the lighted cross on the Colorado mountain, dreaming of a prince's rescue one day. It was more than that. I had been treated with special care all the way back to the days my heart was sick. In those days, even tickling me could get my heart beating in a dangerous way. As a matter of fact, my cousin was pretty sure she *had* killed me after one of those irresistible "goochy-goochy-goo" tickles! I had been treated as fragile, and my new friend Marilyn didn't know the rules!

Scrubbing the grout on the kitchen floor seemed much too Cinderella for me; it's not that I thought I was *above* it, I just hadn't had to *do* it much! Marilyn handed me the sponge, and I got down on that floor! When woodwork needed painting, guess who dusted it off first?!

[15] The Martins. "Stars Below." By Jake Hess Jr. Windows. 2000. CD

Asher had moved into my room during Chuck's last hospital stay; now months later, he was still sleeping with me every night. When I shared with Marilyn that I was praying about what to do, she showed no mercy: "What's to pray about? He's thirteen...he shouldn't be sleeping with his mother!!" Well, OKAY! I adore her. She was and is just what I needed in my life!

The heart healing that took place those days came through tough love, and not just anyone could have delivered it! God had honored my stepping out to ask for help, and in a way faaaaarrr beyond what I'd hoped for or imagined! I'd love to say I'm still enjoying that beautifully redecorated house, but the Lord, through a series of crazy circumstances, moved the boys and me, less than a year later, into a larger home shared with my mother. God graciously used Ed and Marilyn not only to bring healing and revelation to me, but ultimately to help sell my house. I am eternally blessed by them and grateful to them.

Another One Bites the Dust

❧

"I came to with some guy's gum in MY mouth."

Transplant #2 –Fellow Transplant Recipient, Warren Wilcut

Cardiopulmonary Resuscitation: CPR. Every two years we renew our certification at work. It's not new for me. Chuck and I first learned infant CPR when our little Nikolai was born prematurely. It was the requirement for bringing him home with his apnea monitor. When Chuck's heart began to fail, he slept in the living room where he could sit upright to breathe easier. Nik was in his bassinet close by. There were many nights I stood over that little baby, counting the beeps that represented seconds without breaths…waiting for the number at which I was to start CPR… right next to Nikolai was Chuck…*his* heart working at fifteen percent, waiting for heart transplantation. Even after that successful surgery, it ran through my mind many times that perhaps the Lord placed me in a job where my CPR skills would be kept fresh for such a time as to revive my own husband or child.

Every two years…the rules change. "Start with breaths…start with compressions, breathe twice…give five breaths, sweep the mouth…never put your fingers in a person's mouth!!" How are we supposed to remember when it's always evolving?! THIS year the addition was the AED. The Automated External Defibrillator. Without warning, I was back eighteen years; Chuck's eyes crossing, and him slowly collapsing onto the table, and a noise like that of a door slamming. BANG…and he gets the snot shocked out of him! But, I'm strong and I CAN do this.

The training DVD was turned on, and a drum beat played so we'd keep a good pace with our compressions. "Bang, bang, bang, bang." My coworker Sweet Kerry jumped in singing a song that fit the beat perfectly. However "Another One Bites the Dust" just didn't seem like the appropriate song for this occasion…but humor is good! I decided I could do it. I could put the pads on that dummy and shock the snot out of that dying man. I got down on the mat, started the defibrillator, pulled the backs from the pads…and immediately felt sick. I don't want to be "the strongest woman" so-and-so ever knew. Remember the Twila Paris song, "The Warrior Is a Child"? That's how I felt.

With the grace and permission of my friend and supervisor, I put down the pads and left the dummy to his demise…and with any grace for the future, whatever I've seen and done in the past will come back if I need it again in spite of this lack of practice. I got my certification renewed. I pray that I'll NEVER, EVER need to use it…and I thank God for the most amazing group of women with whom I am privileged to work every day. Most of all, I thank Him that He is so gracious as to heal and mend the brokenhearted…my mourning will turn into dancing…there IS a time for that too.

Are There Birthdays in Heaven?

❧

"And when two lovers woo, They still say, 'I love you.' On that you can rely, No matter what the future brings...As Time Goes By."

Hupfeld 1931

Those first holidays brought such joy and pain all at once. This was a letter I wrote to my Chuck, March 15, 2013:

My Dearest Chuck,

Over the last days and weeks the pendulum of wonder has swung wide. Do I really think you can hear me or see me? Is that veil between us really as thin as some of my God-fearing, Jesus-loving, cross-wearing friends believe it to be? OR, is it more like Skeptical Sara imagines... you're busy telling your stories, visiting Paul and Moses, singing for Jesus! Maybe you're hanging around with our loved ones. Then there's that thing about "The sleeping shall rise..." and I'm not sure WHO that is...because if you're "absent from the body," then you should be "present with the Lord"...so you can't be in the ground sleeping! So... where are you anyway?! In the event that you DO have Facebook, or as a recent movie portrayed, Gracebook...this is for you.

I wish you were here. I wish I could make you lemon bars and not burn them. I wish you could see how lovely our home is becoming. You always wanted it to be more grown-up and less...hand-me-down! You should see all the decorating the Guthmanns have done! I wish you could see your boys turning into men…even Asher. You would be so proud of them. I wish I could hear you sing "Gentle Savior" again and see that standing ovation. I wish I could hear you tell your story, make people laugh and then cry, and lead them to Jesus. I wish I could play cards with you, or Taboo…we always beat the pants off other couples in that! I wish you could snuggle me in the Jacuzzi…er, I mean, pray in the prayer closet every night gazing at the stars. I wish I could hear you sing harmony next to me in church the most.

I hope you are eating all the seafood your heart desires. I love you with all my broken heart. Happy forty-sixth! You would have been older this six months…I'd have had to submit! Love, Your Sara

I'm including that personal love letter for this reason…because I know I am not the only one who asks the questions I asked above. Scripture is True, and if God cannot lie (Numbers 23:19), He cannot be inconsistent. Absent from the body = present with God (2 Corinthians 5:6-8). Sleeping = dead… will Rise = they weren't there already (1 Thessalonians 4:16)! Digging into His Word often reveals great understanding…BUT some things remain a mystery…at least to me! Time is one of those things. I've yet to decide what I believe about that "thin veil" between us and those who've gone before. I don't yet know if Chuck ever watches us, or if he's talking to my dad and sister who are "there" too…or if his spirit is alive but he has no body…What I DO know is…because Jesus lives, Chuck lives…and I will live!

No More Night

⌘

"Slowly, the names from the Book are read. I know the King,
so there's no need to dread. No more night, no more pain.
No more tears, never crying again. Praises to the Great I Am,
we will live in the light of the Risen Lamb."[16]

David Phelps

Good Friday always makes me pensive…for the obvious reasons. Jesus became my Savior when I was just seven years old, and by His grace we remained friends throughout my growing up years. I remember thinking He came into my heart through that VSD hole, and patched it Himself! Actually, it was Easter time about one year after Chuck received his new heart that I closed my heart for the first time since I'd been a little girl.

Years of Easter celebrations took place before our relationship was totally restored. One Easter, Chuck and I were visiting a church where we were scheduled to minister later that evening. Things were not going well for the worship team; something we musicians refer to as a "train wreck"! Suddenly, the pastor ran onto the platform waving his arms and shouting, "The enemy is trying to ROB us of our worship!!!"

Chuck and I gave a little glare at the boys, who were elementary school age…one of those parental looks that says, "Ssshh…don't make a peep!

---

[16] Phelps, David. "No More Night." By Walt Harrah. No More Night: David Phelps Live in Birmingham. Word Records. 2007

185

Pretend this happens everywhere!!" Eventually it was our turn on stage and we "did our thing" like always, my part almost a rote act by then. Another Easter, I told my story of anger at God, and pleaded with the congregation to allow Jesus to reveal His perfect love and plan in their lives. Still, it was another Easter I was unwilling to do that for myself. A few years later, Easter morning at yet another church around the corner where we were blessed to sing and speak, the pastor shortened the offering hymn to save time. You just can't DO that with some hymns! We had "Crucified My Lord," "Nailed Him to the Tree," and "Laid Him in the Tomb"...but He'd never yet "Rose Up from the Grave"! Sometimes THAT causes me to tremble, tremble, tremble!!

Humor aside, there were seven years of singing and speaking into people's lives that I now know the Holy Spirit was using to woo me back into His arms. The word of my testimony spoken over and over began to convince even myself that His love was bigger than my pain and disappointment. His sovereignty is what my heart desired...still desires...and I will not find offense in it. Before this, God's plan so offended me and hurt that I felt He had abandoned me and did not love me; He allowed so many trials which we endured.

Now, I *know* His love every day and *know* He is carrying me through, even though I hurt and miss my Chuck so much. I don't always FEEL it, but I *know* it. I trust His will unfolds though I don't know what it is... and in recent days what I did know of it seems to be changing! Still, I am convinced that "neither death nor life, neither angels nor demons, neither the present nor the future, nor any powers, neither height nor depth, nor anything else in all creation will be able to separate me from the love of God that is in Christ Jesus our Lord!" (Romans 8:38-39).

The same goes for you, Dear Friends. Jewish, Catholic, Presbyterian, gay, pew-jumper, or choosing atheism, there is a God who loves you so much, who sent His Son and who has made a way for you to live in freedom, now and always. You don't have to change to meet Him. You don't have to worry about a bunch of rules, contrary to popular belief. Find a congregation, or a family who will help you *be who you are* while you learn to walk with God and *who He is*. You were made in His image and are a thread in a beautiful tapestry being woven for this day and time. You are not an accident. You have value...so much that a real Person suffered a terrible torturous death, even though He was powerful enough to let that plan of God go undone. He is Jesus, and He is risen again. Easter Sunday, we celebrate the resurrection that not only allows His presence to be with us now, but will someday let me see my Chuck again!

I Forgive, Help My Unforgiveness

⌖

The following is a letter I wrote Fall of 2013. I never received a response, so assume it was circular filed. As the first anniversary of this day drew near, the memory rehearsed over and over in my mind. THIS was my call to forgive.

Dear B. A. Fire Department,

On March 16, 2011, you were called to my home as my husband had become very ill. Three techs arrived, entered our bedroom, and stood at the end of the bed questioning Chuck. "How are you, Sir?" No response.

"Sir, can you hear me?"

My mother and I explained, "Chuck is a heart transplant recipient of seventeen years and was recently diagnosed and treated for cancer."

"Sir, do you think you've got the flu?" No response.

"Sir, do you think you need to go to the hospital?" No response.

Again, I explained the seriousness of his condition and history. "Yes, he needs to go."

Over and over you questioned him…asking him if he needed to go to the hospital, or if he thought he had the flu. Not once did anyone take his vital signs. Not once did you consider the very serious history that had been mentioned.

"Sir, do you need to go to the hospital?"

My husband finally worked up enough energy to respond in his always the joker way, yet barely audible, "Unless you have a magic wand."

"Sir, we don't have a magic wand…do you need to go to the hospital?"

SERIOUSLY? What the hell were you thinking? Were we interrupting your game of Rummy? Perhaps you were missing your favorite episode of Gunsmoke and could not be bothered. Is it really your job to diagnose the flu? After ten minutes of questions which were practically shouted at Chuck, you finally agreed to take him. I watched as he was loaded into the red ambulance and then followed you out of the neighborhood in my own car. I'm guessing you took the scenic route or stopped by QT for a Coke as I had time to take my mother all the way to her home, drop her off, and still pull into St. Francis DIRECTLY behind you. You were in no hurry.

My husband nearly died that day. Within just a short time from arriving at the hospital, he was diagnosed with septic shock, put on a ventilator, and I was told to call in our three children to say good-bye.

Over the years, it has been routine for my kids and me to pray every time a fire truck or ambulance passes our way. We pray for the patient inside, and we pray for the medical team and driver to have wisdom and safety as they maneuver the streets against normal traffic signals. So the reason I am writing you now is that I need to forgive you. For the last year, seeing your ambulance did not evoke a prayer in my heart, but a knot in my stomach; and I wondered what TV show you were begrudgingly missing…I wondered if you were frustrated with your patient for interrupting your dinner…I haven't prayed for your safety, only for the patient inside who may not survive due to your lack of care. I hate that feeling. I hate thinking that about anyone at all. I forgive you for your lack of service that day. When I see your trucks go by, I will no longer entertain the thoughts that come to mind…though it may take some time before they stop COMING to mind. I choose to forgive. I choose, again, to pray for you AND your patients from now on.

By God's grace, my husband lived another 15 months after that day you came. He is in Heaven now, and we choose to continue living out our stories here until our time to be with him again comes.

Sincerely,

Sara Stophel

Sending that letter did indeed bring a sort of closure to the pain of that dreadful day. I can attest to the fact that I now AM able to pray without anger when I see a Broken Arrow fire truck. God, in His infinite wisdom, knew what I'd need to heal and forgive: Writing. He knows what you need too. He knows how to take the pain and anger you've lived and evolve it into grace and healing. Put it before Him as an opportunity to express His love to you and through you. Forgiveness provides for healing.

Gonna Need a New Robe

❧

"...for He has clothed me with garments of salvation
and arrayed me in a robe of righteousness...."

Isaiah 61:10

One morning following Chuck's address change, the doorbell rang...
LATE morning...11:00 a.m. Everyone was sound asleep after a late
night of hot-tubbing and movies. Zoltan barked and barked at the door,
and I quickly checked my text messages to make sure I was not due to
be anywhere. WHEW...but then Creston answered the door. It was my
longtime friend, homeschool mentor, baby-sitting co-op'er Melissa, with
an iced coffee in hand! She graciously came to make sure I was out of bed
and pulling through another day; however, when Creston told me he had
answered the door, I panicked!

I don't own a robe...and my robe of righteousness was nowhere to
be found! Worse, the previous night I had trouble finding my family-safe
PJs, so I was sleeping in an oversized black T-shirt that reads "BI*CH
ON WHEELS." Being the mother of the year that I am...I just as well
tell you that my Creston MADE me that shirt following the many weeks
and months of advocating for my husband (and previously for my daddy)
with hospital professionals!! Ever need a patient advocate...I'm your girl!
SO...there I was, profanity-laden T-shirt, barely conscious at 11:00 a.m.,
telling my son to lie to a Church Board Member's wife. "Tell her I'm in the
shower!!" Not my finest moment, and I was certain that SHE was certain

that was a lie! I have since asked her forgiveness and thanked her for the yummy treat!

Two years out from my days of advocacy...the opportunity arose to, again, make use of that "B on W" title! There's a certain cellular phone company with which we held a contract for five phones. After things settled down a bit, I took the Certificate of Death to the local branch to request one contract be canceled as the person who used that line was DEAD. Who knew that would be so difficult. Several visits, calls, and discussions later, I ran out of fight; they won...I paid for Chuck's phone another 20 months, eventually giving his line to my mother. At least she could use it to play Solitaire while we paid out the contract.

With time I got my fight back! I spoke with a local store manager who, again, was unable to do anything for me. Even though they advertised my exact phone package for $160/month, I would have to continue paying twice that much due to Chuck's having had a business account; adding insult to injury, when my phone rang at home, Caller-ID displayed, in large, big screen letters..."Chuck Stophel is calling!" Sigh. In order to remove his name and change from a business account, I'd owe a mere $1,300.00 deposit due to my lack of credit...house owned by my parents, cars paid in full, no credit cards...at least Dave Ramsey would be proud!

This is how I left the store that day...in a very calm, but slightly louder than necessary voice..."Thank you, Jerry, for your help. I realize this is not your fault. Let me just be sure I understand...after paying for my DEAD HUSBAND'S PHONE for nearly two years (at which time every eye in the store turned my way), I am still unable to remove his name, and have to continue paying twice as much as you advertise, because we have a business account without having a business? Have I understood that correctly? The company for which you work has no policy or concern for a young(ish) widow with three children? Have I got that right?" (Interrupting his embarrassed nod), "OKAY, thank you. You should look forward to hearing from Channel 6."

By the time I reached my car I was shaking. But, you know what's amazing? They suddenly discovered a way to wave all of the deposit fees, change the names on the account, AND make it a personal account at the lesser price! Yes, they heard from the local news station's producer... unfortunately, it took that. But, another milestone was taken. I had to get help, but it got done! Those were the things Chuck took care of, and now I had stepped out of my comfort zone to do what nobody else could do! Totally gonna sleep in that black T-shirt whenever I need some umph to fight...hopefully my righteous robe will shine through from under there somewhere!

Healing came through stepping out and trusting in the fight.

A Tempest of Emotions

❦

*"Poetry is when an emotion has found its thought
and the thought has found words."*

Frost 1874-1963

They say (whomever THEY are) that grieving takes a year. Now three years out, yes, it's easier. I still grieve though. Some days my heart hurts for its own loss, and other days for the loss my boys suffer. The following, though, was written on our twenty-fourth wedding anniversary, one year after Chuck's change of address.

July 16, 2013

Sometimes I find myself in a tempest of emotions. Feelings of sadness and joy, jealousy and gratefulness, all whirling around in my head and surely to collide at some point possibly leaving casualties. July 16th marks both my twenty-fourth wedding anniversary and the day we honored the life of my Chuck after he left the earth. He is constantly in my thoughts. And dreams…day and night, and I miss him tremendously. Sad.

At the same time, I have been so blessed this week hearing stories from friends who have just returned from the mission field. God is doing fantastic things in other parts of the world to reveal Himself as the One True God! JOY!

Then, there is a couple I know and love dearly whom God has blessed in such a special way that they are now able to work together, and that, at one of my favorite schools on earth. I'm so thrilled for them. Still, they get each other, and they get that school…and it all makes me want to SQUEEZE them just a little too tightly. Jealous.

Finally and most importantly because it's of eternal value, my feelings of gratefulness come in the form of tears much like all the other feelings; these, though, are happy tears! Today, I heard confirmation that two of my Little Ones from class received Jesus as their Lord. Could there BE anything more precious than a little girl praying, "I'm sorry…come into my heart." OR, another who, though she is mostly nonverbal, told me with her electronic "talker" that she had prayed to Jesus at our mini Garden of Gethsemane in the room!? Grateful! Emotional tempest!

What a fantastic Creator we serve! How great it is that our circumstances don't have to determine our joy! We can experience joy even while grieving because it comes from Him and is deeper than the loss. What a tender heart He must have to make us such that we are able to feel so deeply, both the joys and the pains. One helps make the other so much sweeter.

I Need My Sara-Tonin!

❧

"When I lift up my head, He lifts up my heart
and my troubles just all roll away."[17]

Dottie Rambo

That's the catchy tune we sang every Monday night to close our barbershop quartet rehearsal. Those lyrics ran through my mind over and over one week; however, my troubles were NOT rollin' away. With every minute I was less certain things would work out.

Come to find...there's a stroooong correlation between one day's complete loss of perspective and the four or five days I forgot to take my happy pills!! Whoever said depression is all in your head was completely right... my head cannot see beyond the immediate without medicine. Very apparent. Twenty-three years with an amazing husband, wonderful children, and a deep – albeit rocky on days – relationship with Jesus, didn't cancel out fear of being left alone to raise three boys, hundreds of thousands in bills (thankfully we had great insurance!), and the reality that God does not always work in the way we hope and pray.

Remember, reality caused a collision in my faith. As a Christian woman, I was supposed to trust the Lord with my future...heck...I often struggled trusting Him with my present! Laughter and music filled our house; meanwhile I'd stare at my cupboards full of food and see no potential for a meal.

---

[17] Rambo, Dottie. "When I Lift Up My Head." By Dottie Rambo. Gaither Homecoming. 2004.

For ten years I told Chuck, "Something's *wrong* with me." I didn't sleep more than two or three hours in a row for more years than I can count. Christians think depression means a lack of faith or a distrust in God... some would even accuse a person of having sin in his/her life that is causing that depression. As a matter of fact, I spoke at a women's retreat, sharing transparently about dealing with fear. Afterwards a lady scolded me for "confessing fear" in my life. I asked her if she had never experienced fear... Her response was that she occasionally had CONCERNS or thinks about what MIGHT happen. MY response: "That, my Dear...is semantics!" That was the end of our conversation! Hear me, Gals (and Guys!), if there are times when your brain needs a little boost of serotonin or melatonin...it's OKAY!

So with springtime comes a list of tough anniversaries, and a slew of decisions for the coming year. Each year so far, God has come through with direction. So far, I've stayed working for Little Light House. Each year He has given wisdom and then provided for Asher's education. I'll probably still get a little antsy when April comes around...but more and more I know in my KNOWER that God will do His part to lead and guide. If I find myself lying on my bed, imagining myself disassembled like a mannequin awaiting her stylist...I now assume I've missed a few doses of happy pills! It is what it is. God using medicine to help deal and heal!

YOUR TURN

Precedence is a good way to discover what God's will might be in a particular instance. I'll admit, I'm not that good at it yet, but my hope is to be much better versed in God's Word, so that when a situation arises, I can find a similar precedence in the Bible. No, there won't be exact problems to compare and contrast, but I think there will be examples close enough that we can learn from them, along with praying that we hear His direction! Below, jot down a time when precedence made it easy for you to trust God, or...like me...afraid to trust too much.

_____

_____

_____

_____

_____

Ask the Lord to bring to your remembrance anyone with whom you have unforgiveness in your heart. Allow Him to help you forgive. Write a note to that person expressing your true feelings, how you were offended, and then, whether or not it's ever sent...make clear your forgiveness. Remember the prayer Jesus taught His disciples..."Forgive us our sins, just as we have forgiven those who have sinned against us" (Matthew 6:12 TLB).

_____

_____

_____

_____

_____

_____

A Song of Purpose

Because It's True

❧

"I want to live my life in the presence of Jesus, as if He were in my view... As if He were all I knew, and as if He had brought me through...Only Because It's True."[18]

Ron Harris

How is it that people get through heart transplants, cancer, divorce, job loss, abuse...life on this planet, without having hope? Really. I'm asking. Maybe you are reading this because you knew Chuck, or know me, and you're just being supportive. Maybe God is just religion to you. How do you face so much uncertainty without hope that something bigger than yourself is at work in the universe? How do you live in this fallen world without believing there is Someone bigger than yourself who loves you, and has a plan for good and not calamity? (See Jeremiah 29:11.) What do you do to recover from the grief of thinking you'll never, ever see your loved one again once he or she is gone? Even with all of my doubt and anger toward God and His ways…I always knew there was nothing better, nothing else. I knew I had to come to a point of trust again because this world does not offer me anything of value.

My most favorite book, after the Bible, is *The Shack* by William Paul Young[19]. It changed my life. There was a bit of controversy about it, even being called heresy by a close pastor friend...though I do not think he ever

---

[18]Chrisco, Sue. "Because It's True." By Ron Harris. The Singer. 1983. LP.
[19]Young, William Paul. "The Shack." Windblown Media, 2008.

read it himself! *The Shack* is a novel...a story. It is not true, but there is so much truth in the fiction. I love how Pastor Buskirk explained it..."God tangibilitates." That being, He demonstrates Himself as His characteristics, right at our point of need. When we need a healer, God is Jehovah Rapha. When we need provision, God is Jehovah Jireh. When we wonder if He even knows what we are going through, He reminds us He is El Roi, the God who Sees. God makes Himself tangible.

In *The Shack,* God is portrayed as an Aunt Jemima-type black woman. Not biblically accurate, I realize, but the main character, Mack, grew up with an abusive earthly father and would not have related well to God as a loving Father. At one point in the story, when Mack is angry and frustrated at the Great Sadness that has taken place in his life, God tells him, "Just because I work incredible good out of unspeakable tragedies doesn't mean I *orchestrate* the tragedies. Don't ever assume that My *using* something means I *caused* it or that I *need* it to accomplish My purposes. That will only lead you to false notions about Me. Grace doesn't depend on suffering to exist, but where there is suffering you will find grace in many facets and colors." I LOVE that. And I know there are a zillion others who would find healing in that phrase. He doesn't NEED cancer, or diabetes, or job loss, or divorce, to demonstrate His grace and purpose. He just USES them to bring redemption to our broken lives. He IS good. That took years for me to say.

Every day I go to work and see beautiful kiddos who were born with disabilities of all kinds. Some are blind, or deaf, or have extra chromosomes. Some, short of God's intervention, will never talk or walk, even under the care of talented therapists, while others will catch up with their peers and develop into productive "typical" people in society. All of them have purpose and bring joy to their homes. All of them! Still, their parents are only being honest when they wonder why their babies have to face such challenges. Even in the Bible, Jesus' best friends asked Him about a blind man they'd seen walking down the street. "Rabbi, who sinned: this man or his parents, that he was born blind?" Jesus' answer was that they were asking the *wrong* question. He told his friends, instead of asking for someone on which to place blame, look instead for what God could DO in and through that blind man! (John 9:1-5). Turns out the power of God was beautifully revealed through that man's life. Redemption.

Throughout my life, I have put God on trial. I have blamed Him for not healing my sister, for allowing Chuck to have cancer – twice...for not answering prayers that I'd asked in faith. I have been a lot like The Shack's main character, Mack. He, in his pain, blamed God for not intervening on behalf of his little girl. But what Papa (God in the story) shows Mack and what God has to remind me, is that we do not know the whole story. Mack did not know about all the past generations of abuse in his own family or in the family of his daughter's perpetrator. He wanted God to punish the bad person. So Papa asks how far back to go with the punishing...because sin is rooted in history. Should He punish just the bad guy, or go one generation back into *his* history...or two generations back...or three? He would have to go all the way back to Adam and Eve, which is, in fact, what He did. He allowed them free will. He allowed them the opportunity for perfection; life walking face-to-Face with God. They chose the sin of pride...with all they had, they wanted more...to be LIKE God, knowing good and evil. It caused them to be removed from His presence...BUT, He didn't leave it there. The story wasn't over! He provided a Savior through Jesus. Thank You, God!

I do not know the whole story either. I do not know how many lives have been touched and changed and brought to His Kingdom through Chuck's gracious living even while suffering. I cannot calculate what Kingdom building has happened over the years due to Chuck's willingness to submit to God's sovereign plans for his earthly life. For me, submission had to change from being about *authority* and *obedience* to being about my RELATIONSHIP with Jesus. A relationship of love and respect (as described in *The Shack*). I'm getting there! More and more I'm able to look at situations from God's perspective, even when I'm not sure of the outcome. It's taken a loooong time, and I'm far from there...but as 1 Corinthians 1:18 says, "The message of the cross is power to those of us who are BEING saved." It's a process. I'm still under construction. Had I the opportunity to do it all over again, I hope I would sooner choose submission to sovereignty. I hope I'd be better at trusting God with the "little foxes." I hope He would have more opportunity to shine in and through me to those around. However, I sure do hope and pray I never get to prove I'd do better the second...or third time around!

If sovereignty has trumped your faith...if you have done all to stand, and then witnessed your story move in a direction you never thought or prayed it would go, you are not alone. There are so many of us! Please hear me, God loves you. He's actually crazy about you. He's twiddling His thumbs, awaiting your ear to hear His heart. Ask Him to show up in a tangible way. Tell Him you need Him to tangibilitate! Absolutely, "Blessed are those who have not seen and yet have believed" (John 20:29). But, HEALED are those of us who believe because He revealed Himself to us at our point of need. (That's not scripture; that's Sara's experience.) THAT experience has healed *my* heart. I love the old hymn, Blessed Assurance, by Frances Crosby..."This is my story, this is my song...praising my Savior all the day long!" It has been a long time in coming!

Blessed assurance, Jesus is mine!
Oh, what a foretaste of glory divine!

Heir of salvation, purchase of God,
Born of His Spirit, washed in His blood.

Refrain: This is my story, this is my song,
Praising my Savior all the day long;
This is my story, this is my song,
Praising my Savior all the day long[20].

What's your story? Where has God trumped your hopes and dreams for His better and higher ways? How do you need Him to tangibilitate? Tell your story, even if you haven't got the whole thing figured out yet. Like Chuck's favorite passage in the Bible...our stories create readiness, nudging people toward receptive insight. Our stories create readiness...even in ourselves! Thank you for reading *my* story. I pray that Jesus has been made real in you and to you.

END

---

[20] Crosby, Frances J. "Blessed Assurance." Public Domain. 1873.

YOUR TURN

You're going to need more space...but here's a starting point! Congratulations...you are on your way to a whole and healed truster!!

Lord, here is MY story. Use it for Your glory! _____

_____

_____

_____

_____

_____

_____

_____

_____

_____

About the Author

Sara Stophel is a writer, speaker, and full-time mom. She works part time outside her home, but leaves time for nightly family games and writing. Along with her late husband, Chuck, Sara spent many years traveling, singing, and telling the story of God's sovereignty colliding with her bigger-than-mustard-seed-sized faith!

She loves to laugh, watch movies that keep her awake thinking, and push right up to the line where cute and unbecoming meet! Sara and her three sons make their home in Tulsa, Oklahoma.

A NOTE FROM THE AUTHOR

Thank you for taking the time to read my story, *Trumped by Sovereignty.* If this book has helped you, moved you, or touched your life...even if it made you a little cranky...I would love to hear from you!

You may contact me at:
Email: saragraph918@gmail.com

LOOKING FOR AN INSPIRATIONAL SPEAKER
FOR YOUR UPCOMING EVENT?

If you have an upcoming women's conference, or know of a school, church or business looking for an inspirational speaker who can make the audience both laugh, cry and walk away inspired let us know.

Sara is available to speak in your area,
please email her at the address above.